I0807032

Cover page:
Robert Lepage in **The Andersen Project.**
Photo: Érick Labbé

Endpaper:
Indoor low angle shot of Caserne fire station tower.
Photo: Jacques Plante

Ex Machina
Artistic Director/ Robert Lepage
Production Manager/ Martine Rochon
Project Manager/ Ève-Alexandra Saint-Laurent

Graphic Design/ Paquebot Design

Note: The titles of the theatre works listed in the Theatrography (p. 82) are printed in boldface in the vignettes.

The following individuals collaborated in the writing of this book:
Lynda Beaulieu, Micheline Beaulieu, Michel Bernatchez, Joëlle Cloutier, Jean-Sébastien Côté, Félix Dagenais, Carl Fillion, Bernard Foccroulle, Richard Fréchette, Marie Gignac, Tobie Horswill, Louise Roussel, Jean-Pierre Vézina and Neilson Vignola

Special thanks to:
François Barbeau, Robert Caux, David-Alexandre Chabot, Esther Charron, Mira Cliche, Jacques Collin, Yves Dubé, Yves Fillion, Ludovic Fouquet, Michel Gauthier, Sophie Grenier, Claudel Huot, Jean Lebourdais, David Leclerc, Jacques Lessard, Hélène Marcaurelle, Marc Marnie, Pedro Pirès, Jacques Plante, Gilles Tapie, Truong Chanh Trung, Emmanuel Valette, Big Brother Productions (New York), Metropolitan Opera (New York), Royal Opera House – Covent Garden (London), Scène Éthique, Théâtre Royal de la Monnaie (Brussels), Ville de Québec and Bengt Wanselius

Ex Machina website: www.lacaserne.net

No part of this book, covered by the copyright hereon, may be reproduced or used in any form or by any means–graphic, electronic or mechanical – without prior permission of the publisher, except for excerpts in a review. Any request for photocopying of any part of this book shall be directed in writing to Access Copyright (The Canadian Copyright Licensing Agency), 1 Yonge Street, Suite 800, Toronto, Ontario, Canada M5E 1E5; tel.: (416) 868-1620; fax: (416) 868-1621.

Copyright © 2007 Patrick Caux and Bernard Gilbert
Translation copyright © 2009 Neil Kroetsch

Talonbooks
P.O. Box 2076, Vancouver, British Columbia, Canada V6B 3S3
www.talonbooks.com

Printed and bound in Canada.
First Printing: 2009

Talonbooks gratefully acknowledges the financial support of the Canada Council for the Arts; the Government of Canada through the Book Publishing Industry Development Program; and the Province of British Columbia through the British Columbia Arts Council and the Book Publishing Tax Credit for our publishing activities.

Ex Machina: From Page to Stage was originally published in French by Les éditions du Septentrion in 2007. We acknowledge the financial support of the Government of Canada through the National Translation Program for Book Publishing, for our translation activities.

Library and Archives Canada Cataloguing in Publication

Caux, Patrick
Ex Machina: from page to stage / Patrick Caux & Bernard Gilbert; translated by Neil Kroetsch.

Translation of: Ex Machina: chantiers d'écriture scénique.
Includes bibliographical references.
ISBN 978-0-88922-617-3

1. Ex Machina (Theater company). 2. Theater – Québec (Province). 3. Performing arts – Québec (Province). I. Gilbert, Bernard, 1958- II. Kroetsch, Neil III. Title.

PN2306.Q4C3813 2009 792.06'0714 C2009-902842-5

EX MACHINA

FROM PAGE TO STAGE

PATRICK CAUX / BERNARD GILBERT
TRANSLATED BY NEIL KROETSCH

TALONBOOKS

Erotic fantasy scene. **Zulu Time.** (Jinny Jessica Jacinto and Marco Poulin) Photo: Reggie Tucker

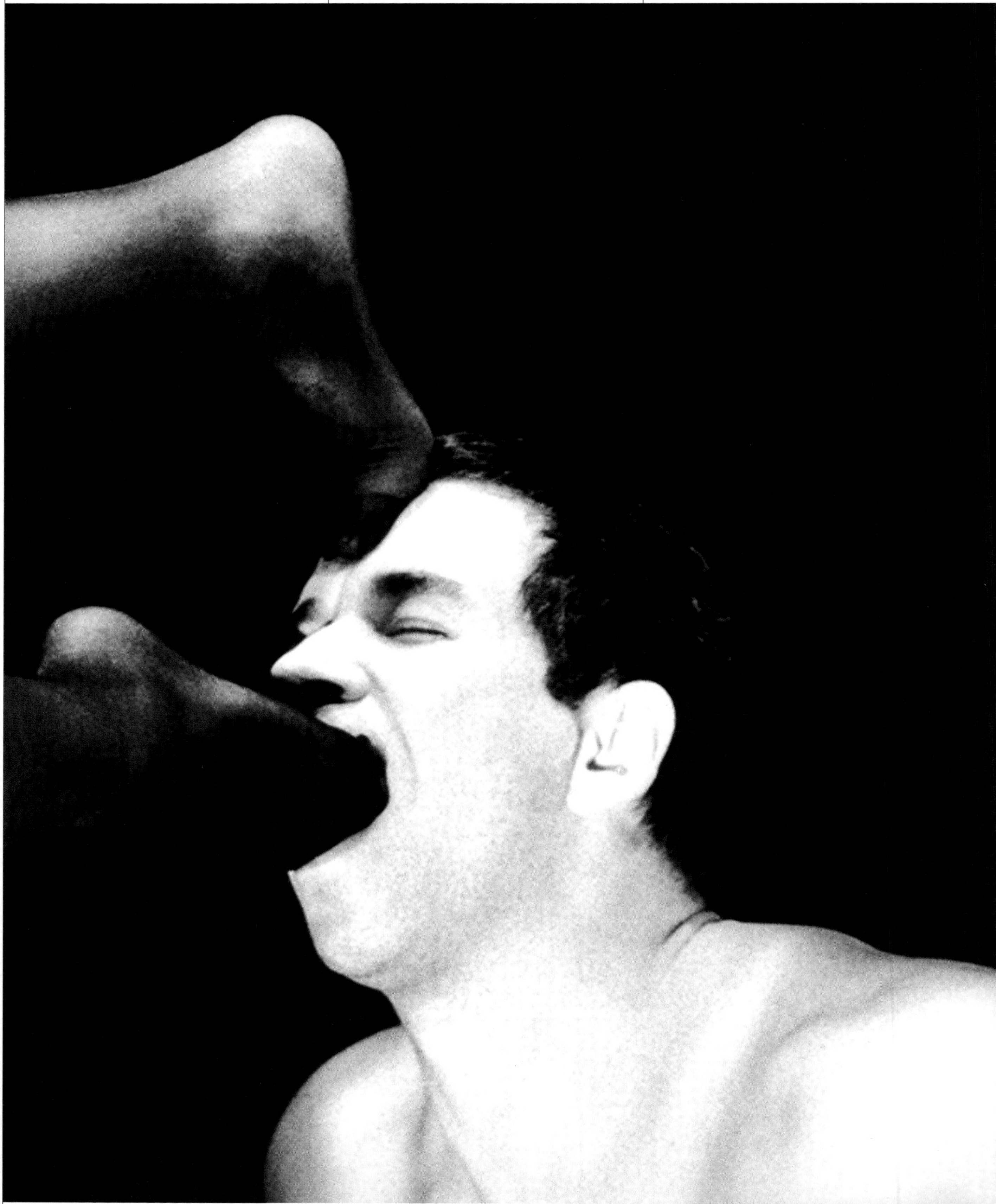

SIDEBARS

Upstairs washroom in a building in New York.
The Seven Streams of the River Ota.
(Michel F. Côté, Richard Fréchette, Normand Daneau, Patrick Goyette and Réjean Vallée)
Photo: Claudel Huot

FOREWORD

Ex Machina is a creative arts company that works simultaneously on a multitude of highly diverse projects. Its dynamism and its relentless search for new forms of story-telling mean that it must move quickly from one project draft to another, without ever really having the time to reread a script or stop to take stock of its approach and working methods.

This book is a sort of thinking-out-loud reflection on an exciting journey that has been full of radiant discoveries, as well as intriguing byways where we often found ourselves stuck. The collective creative process that is Ex Machina is based mainly on intuition. There is no recipe or set of instructions but, by dint of experimentation, we have come to realize that there might be an underlying philosophy or attitude, or at least a different way to approach things.

This book does not claim to propose any new theories, but is simply an attempt to understand how, through our processes, we have been able to integrate other existing approaches. Touring these plays and operas extensively has turned the creators and performers into privileged witnesses to new forms of theatre, onlookers who understand that theatre, like the world itself, evolves very rapidly, as do its practitioners and its audiences. The influence of film and television and the new dramaturgical possibilities offered by multimedia have turned narrative conventions upside down, opening the way to new forms of expression and new languages of staging that have only barely been explored. It is thus not simply the content and form of theatre that are being called into question by Ex Machina, but also the role that theatre will play in the new exchange of ideas in the 21st century.

ROBERT LEPAGE

Trailer scene.
Lipsynch. (Nuria Garcia)
Photo: Érick Labbé

Part 1 / In Search of New Connections, New Mutations

BY PATRICK CAUX

FROM QUEBEC CITY TO TOKYO BY WAY OF NEW YORK, LONDON OR MOSCOW, EX MACHINA INVITES AUDIENCES THE WORLD OVER TO THEATRICAL EXPERIMENTS WHERE TECHNOLOGY IS PART OF THE HUMAN ADVENTURE. ONSTAGE, HIERARCHIES, WORKING METHODS AND NARRATIVE CODES ARE TURNED TOPSY-TURVY IN ORDER TO CREATE A RICH STAGE VOCABULARY THAT IS FREE OF CONSTRAINTS.

The East seduces the West.
Red Dragon.
The Dragons' Trilogy.
Second version.
(Emily Shelton and
Jean-Antoine Charest)
Photo: Érick Labbé

In 1993 when Robert Lepage suggested to his colleagues that a specific identity and image be found for his next working group, he imposed one condition. The word "theatre" was not to be part of the name of the new company.

That condition is indicative of the spirit motivating the troupe. Its approach is aimed at breaking down barriers, dismantling conventions, knocking received ideas off their pedestals and inventing a stage language very much attuned to its time and place.

"The artists of Ex Machina believe that theatre craves new sources of inspiration," notes Michel Bernatchez, the company's producer. "What is needed is a commingling of the performing arts such as dance, opera and music with the recording arts such as cinema, video and multimedia. It calls for encounters between scientists and playwrights, between scenic artists and architects, between artists from Quebec and artists from elsewhere."

"This intermingling would give rise to new artistic forms. That was the gamble that Ex Machina took – to become a laboratory, an incubator of a theatre capable of connecting with a 21st century audience."

This desire to create new theatrical forms and languages is the result of insatiable curiosity about all things human. Each piece created by Ex Machina contains in its artistic approach a reaching out to the other, a search for the other, a desire to encounter others.

Prior to founding the company, a taste for other people and other places was already a constant in the projects of Robert Lepage. His prologue to *The Dragons' Trilogy* foreshadowed the works to come. In the darkness, the silence is broken by a woman's voice. "Je ne suis jamais allée en Chine." The phrase is immediately repeated in English by a man. "I've never been to China," and then in Cantonese by another man.

For many observers, *The Dragons' Trilogy* expanded the horizons of Quebec theatre. For the first time, a Quebec production toured abroad, "telling our tales by approaching the other." The playwright Michel Tremblay wrote of the piece that "for me it was an utter revelation, or as the Americans would say an epiphany, a major work of capital importance. After fighting for the right to be a citizen of my own country, I suddenly found myself to be a citizen of the world."[1]

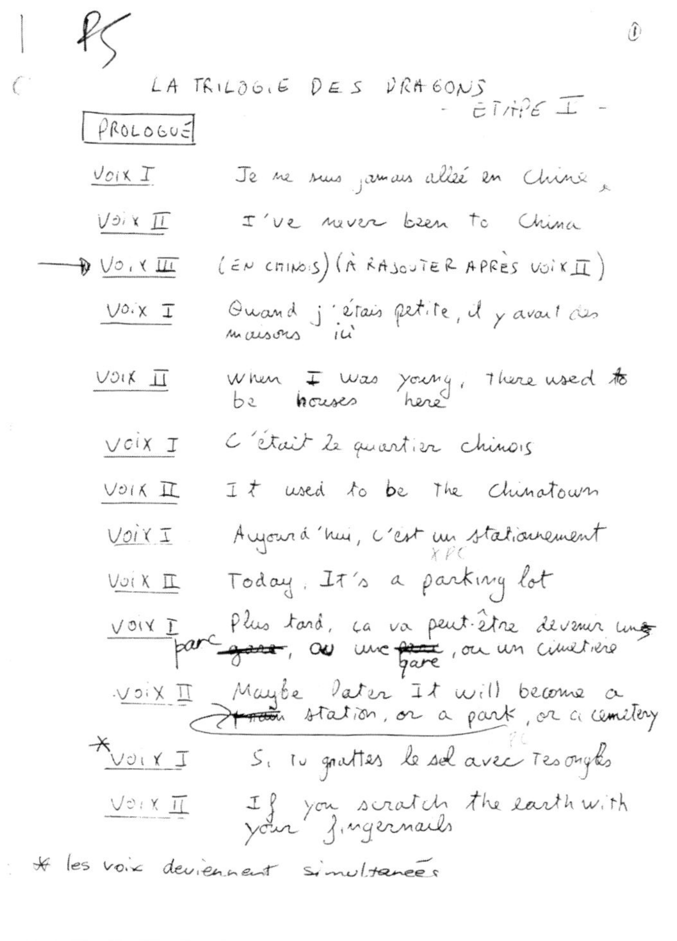

PS ①

LA TRILOGIE DES DRAGONS
- ÉTAPE I -

PROLOGUE

VOIX I Je ne suis jamais allée en Chine
VOIX II I've never been to China
VOIX III (EN CHINOIS) (À RAJOUTER APRÈS VOIX II)
VOIX I Quand j'étais petite, il y avait des maisons ici
VOIX II When I was young, there used to be houses here
VOIX I C'était le quartier chinois
VOIX II It used to be the Chinatown
VOIX I Aujourd'hui, c'est un stationnement
VOIX II Today, It's a parking lot
VOIX I Plus tard, ça va peut-être devenir un parc, ou une gare, ou un cimetière
VOIX II Maybe later It will become a station, or a park, or a cemetery
*VOIX I Si tu grattes le sol avec tes ongles
VOIX II If you scratch the earth with your fingernails

* les voix deviennent simultanées

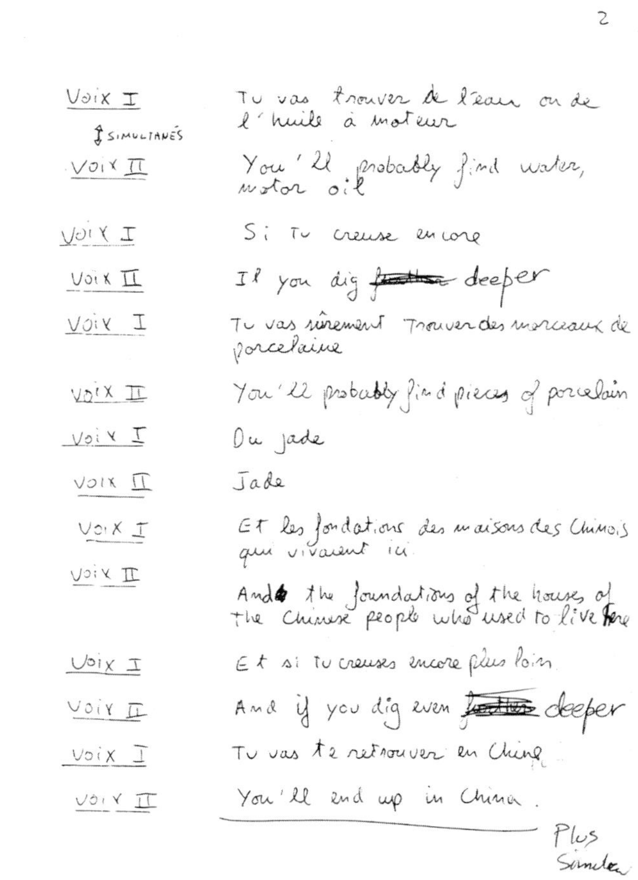

2

VOIX I Tu vas trouver de l'eau ou de l'huile à moteur
SIMULTANÉS
VOIX II You'll probably find water, motor oil
VOIX I Si tu creuse encore
VOIX II If you dig deeper
VOIX I Tu vas sûrement trouver des morceaux de porcelaine
VOIX II You'll probably find pieces of porcelain
VOIX I Ou jade
VOIX II Jade
VOIX I Et les fondations des maisons des Chinois qui vivaient ici
VOIX II And the foundations of the houses of the Chinese people who used to live here
VOIX I Et si tu creuses encore plus loin
VOIX II And if you dig even deeper
VOIX I Tu vas te retrouver en Chine
VOIX II You'll end up in China.

Plus Simulta

Robert Lepage's handwritten prologue.
Marie Gignac's annotations.
The Dragons' Trilogy.
First version.
Archives RLI

More recently, *The Far Side of the Moon*, Lepage's most personal and intimate piece to date, sheds light on the importance of introspection in the company's work. While a desire for new encounters has driven Ex Machina to expand both its physical horizons (by touring) and artistic horizons (through the themes engaged), this desire for the inner journey lies first and foremost at the very heart of its approach.

Now that Ex Machina has toured and performed around the world, Robert Lepage feels compelled to have the driving forces that shape his artistic approach gathered and catalogued in a book.

Like the creative work of Ex Machina, *From Page to Stage* is driven by a double desire for openness and introspection: underpinning this project is our urge to draw a contemporary portrait of the company. To that end, we have decided to describe Ex Machina's artistic approach and some of its sources of inspiration. At the same time, Robert Lepage himself has expressed the wish to embark on more theoretical reflection about the work of Ex Machina so as to discern certain inherent rules underlying the company's work. This is an extraordinary endeavour, for he has traditionally refused to define any creative system, preferring instead to let the methodology of the work assert itself during the course of its various performances.

To facilitate our reflections on indications of a possible theoretical framework behind Ex Machina theatre practice, its director agreed to a number of interviews with the author of this section of the book. The Lepage quotations found in this book are the fruit of those discussions.

1. Michel Tremblay, preface to playscript of *La Trilogie des dragons*, Quebec City, Ex Machina and L'instant même, collection L'instant scène, 2005, p. 8.

The Roots of Ex Machina

TO SET DOWN ROOTS IN THE WORLD OF THE CREATIVE ARTS, EX MACHINA NEEDED A RICH SUBSTRATUM NOURISHED BY TIME, ENCOUNTERS, EXPERIENCES AND DIVERSE SOURCES OF INSPIRATION.

Robert Lepage and Richard Fréchette explore the teachings of Jacques Lecoq as transmitted by Marc Doré.
L'Attaque quotidienne. Théâtre Hummm ...
Photo: Richard Fréchette archives

While at the Conservatoire d'art dramatique in Quebec City, Robert Lepage studied with a mentor who was to influence all his work. "For Marc Doré, theatre was a poetic act first, before being a psychological act. He did not speak of poetry merely as a form of writing, but as a way of moving, of playing."

A worthy heir to the tradition of the Jacques Lecoq school where he himself had studied, Doré pushed his students to be creative. "He gave us the idea, now so central to our work, that the actor is above all a creator. He taught us to observe, to improvise and to play with objects so as to create poetry. In talking to us about Lecoq and the European tradition, he also pushed us to research the root sources of theatre."

Upon leaving the Conservatory in 1978, a group of graduates that included Lepage received a grant to further pursue their studies in Europe. They decided to enrol at the Institut de la personnalité créatrice, directed by Alain Knapp, where the training is arduous, but the actor is taught to channel his energies, to erect barriers when necessary. At the end of a three-week workshop, Robert Lepage and his colleague and friend Richard Fréchette decided to stay in Europe. Their sojourn included a trip to the Avignon Festival.

"It was during that trip that I discovered the Théâtre du Soleil under the direction of Ariane Mnouchkine," recalls Lepage. "We immediately noticed the similarities between her working methods and the method taught by Marc Doré, for the simple reason that she had also studied with Lecoq, so we shared the same theatrical background. It is said that while studying at his school, she was like a sponge. A quiet, retiring student, she would absorb everything Lecoq taught about movement, about mask and clown work. Later she tested everything she had learned, and then transformed and adapted Lecoq's ideas, eventually inventing her own approach. She was quite far ahead of us. At a time when we were discovering the roots of our theatre in Europe, she was researching the Far East – she suspected that the universal sources of theatre, especially as regards the actor's work, were to be found in Asia. She was particularly interested in the codes of Kabuki, Noh theatre, Kathakali, Balinese theatre and the Peking Opera, and starting in the early 1980s she began integrating these traditions into her work."

For Lepage, this was a decisive encounter: Mnouchkine's method put into practice the ideas he had absorbed at the Conservatory. The young artist had discovered a new source of inspiration. "Starting with her first big collective creations in the early 1970s, she placed the actor at the centre of the creative process. She abolished hierarchies within the troupe. For her, each project is allowed to dictate the time required for its full development. A performance is only ready once the troupe has explored all possible avenues. Also, she has her Cartoucherie space, a site dedicated to fleshing out her works. Had I at the time dreamed of founding a company, it would most certainly have been modelled on the Théâtre du Soleil."

Once back home, the two young artists, galvanized by their first sojourn in Europe, founded the Théâtre Hummmm ..., named in honour of the onomatopoeia used by Fred, the renowned author of the *Philémon* comic books. The two associates mounted a few plays, including *L'Attaque quotidienne* (a piece about the tabloid press) and *Saturday Night Taxi*. Lepage took advantage of this period to start directing. It was also during this time that he made the acquaintance of Michel Bernatchez, and he quickly realized that this

Henry IV, directed by Ariane Mnouchkine.
Le Théâtre du Soleil. (M. Durozier, C. Bosc, J. Maurel and G. Freixe)
Photo: Martine Franck

multitalented stage manager had the soul of a builder. Right from their initial projects, the creator and the future producer developed a close working relationship. Bernatchez soon became the organizer whose skills enabled Robert Lepage's many projects to take flight. Even today, it is this close, constant collaboration between artistic aspirations and innovative means of production and financing that allows Ex Machina to create its works in complete freedom.

Ariane Mnouchkine and the Théâtre du Soleil

Ariane Mnouchkine is one of the leading figures of contemporary theatre. After studying with Jacques Lecoq, in 1964 she founded the Théâtre du Soleil with Philippe Léotard. Her theatre is resolutely committed to a collective approach, and profoundly marked by her radical artistic choices. Living literally as a troupe, the approximately 70 actors participate in all company activities, from performing to preparing meals. Everyone is involved in all aspects of the work. This communal approach (all members of the company are paid the same salary) is of course reflected in the construction and presentation of the performances. From collective creations (*1789*, *L'Âge d'or*, *Le Dernier Caravansérail*) to great works in the classic repertory (Aeschylus, Shakespeare, Molière), the Théâtre du Soleil delves into the very origins of theatre and its roots in the Far East. Recent plays have been marked by Asian traditions (Noh, Kabuki, Kathakali, Balinese theatre, Peking Opera, etc.). A worthy heir to Jacques Copeau, Mnouchkine places great importance on words (she frequently collaborates with the writer Hélène Cixous) and on the actors' performance. Her pieces are often supported by the music of Jean-Jacques Lemêtre.

The troupe conducts extensive research for each piece. For example, the company travelled to Asia to immerse themselves in various Oriental traditions prior to creating *Tambours sur la digue*. Using their research as a starting point, they develop worlds into which they invite the audience. Thus the Cartoucherie (the company's home is a former munitions factory in the Bois de Vincennes) is regularly transformed to correspond to the ritual unique to each production. Before the show begins, the audience can watch the actors perform their warm-up exercises or talk to them while there are applying their makeup. To plunge into the spirit of the performance, the spectators can also consult the sources used in creating the piece as they eat a meal (prepared by the members of the troupe) inspired by the region of the world evoked in the production.

Pierre Lamontagne and Yukali.
Two approaches to art.
Dialogue in an art gallery in Vancouver.
White Dragon. **The Dragons' Trilogy.**
3-hour version.
(Robert Lepage and Marie Brassard)
Photo: Claudel Huot

DÉBUT AT LE REPÈRE

For Quebec theatre, the early 1980s was a time of upheaval. Freeing itself from the previous foundational strictures of text, it increasingly gave way to physical theatre whose style and approach were deeply influenced by the performing arts. Young Quebec artists began looking abroad, especially to New York and Berlin, inspired by artists like Laurie Anderson, Robert Wilson and Pina Bausch.

For Lepage, that era was characterized by works such as Gilles Maheu's *L'homme rouge*, the Théâtre Omnibus piece *Beau Monde* and the Michel Lemieux play *L'Oeil rechargeable*. "Those shows were a real break with the past. Within a few years, narrative and aesthetic codes were completely transformed."

It was during that time in Quebec City that Lepage and Fréchette joined the Repère theatre company. One of their former Conservatory teachers, Jacques Lessard, was a founding member, and the entire team shared an interest in creating new works. The company had been inspired by the collective theatre projects of the previous decade, but also nourished by a desire to distance itself from text, telling stories by playing with content and form. Drawing on tangible resources, the company developed its own stage vocabulary and theatrical approach, now renowned across Quebec.

In 1984, Lepage and his associates had their first pan-Canadian success with *Circulations*. "The play was inspired by a road map of the Eastern U.S., its winding roads evoking both the human bloodstream and travel." It also employed stock phrases from old-style English language classes. The critics were bowled over by the piece – highly original, funny, with an allusive tribute to the cinema in its use of low-angle shots. "The concocted image becomes the main character in the performance, with the sound the central element of the dramatic text," intoned one critic in *L'annuaire théâtral*.[2]

2. Marie-Andrée Lamontagne, *Contact, l'encyclopédie de la création*, www.contacttv.net.

A cinematic approach was apparent from the start. Here the illusion of an high angle shot is created onstage.
Circulations. Théâtre Repère.
(Robert Lepage, Lise Castonguay and François Beausoleil)
Photo: Jacques Lessard

The following year, accompanied by Marie Brassard, Jean Casault, Lorraine Côté, Marie Gignac and Marie Michaud, Robert Lepage plunged into the adventure of *The Dragon Trilogy*. In 1987 the team (joined now by the actors Robert Bellefeuille, Richard Fréchette and Yves-Érick Marier) presented the piece in its six-hour version at the Theatre Festival of the Americas. It was an immediate success among audiences and critics alike, launching the young actors onto stages all over the world.
Simultaneously, Lepage was also working on his first solo piece, *Vinci*. Dealing with creation and the role of art, *Vinci* bore the distinctive signature of its author – playing with imagery, reversals of perspective, the importance of symbols, the contrast between the banality of the main character and the genius of Leonardo da Vinci. After a few years with Repère, Lepage had explored the two models that would mark all of his subsequent work – the collective piece and the solo show. *Vinci* was followed in short order by *Polygraph* and *Tectonic Plates*.

Two Chinese sisters, immigrants in Quebec City.
The nostalgia for Asia. Green Dragon. **The Dragons' Trilogy.**
First version. (Marie Brassard and Lorraine Côté)
Photo: Claudel Huot

A woman at the Burger King in Saint-Germain-des-Prés, Paris:
"Ah, so you are a photographer! I myself prefer a warm medium, like painting. A friend once painted my portrait. It was extraordinary! I was in a dry, parched landscape, like something out of a nuclear holocaust. It was a three-quarter face portrait like this. My hands were on my stomach, as though I was carrying the embryo of a new generation of gifted children. And to show that I was the only one who knew, he painted me with an enigmatic smile."
Vinci. (Robert Lepage)
Photo: Claudel Huot

Released from the bonds of gravity. Flight is a recurrent theme in the works of Lepage.
Vinci. (Robert Lepage)
Photo: Claudel Huot

Théâtre Repère

Théâtre Repère was founded in 1980 by Jacques Lessard in conjunction with other actors and artists. The company's mandate was to create "a theatre of images, emotions and characters, theatre teeming with all aspects of performance and of life that moves, that ebbs and flows and that constantly surprises us." In 1978 Jacques Lessard travelled to California to take part in the creative workshops taught by the dancer Ann Halprin of the San Francisco Dancers' Workshop. Her husband, the architect Lawrence Halprin, had developed a method he called RSVP Cycles (Resources, Score, reVised, Performed) that was based on using intuitive creativity to structure the creative process.

Greatly inspired by this method, Lessard devised a theatrical adaptation he called the Cycles Repères. The process is constructed around four words, i.e. resource, sharing, evaluation and performance. The first letters of each French word constitute the word "repère" or point of reference. The company members start by using free improvisation to build characters and to create scenes and situations using ordinary materials as inspiration. "The great innovation of the Cycles," according to Lessard, "lies in the notion of architecture applied to theatre, creating from something concrete. That was what made Théâtre Repère different from the collective creations of the previous decade, where the springboard for creating new work was ideas."[3]

3. Ludovic Fouquet, *Robert Lepage, l'horizon en images*, L'instant même, collection L'instant scène, 2005, p.15.

In developing these first projects, Lepage and his collaborators were soon confronted with the limitations of the company's approach. While there were indeed some extremely rich aspects to the Repère cycles, the method could become a restrictive dogma rather than an organic tool adaptable to the demands of each piece. In the late 1980s Lepage and Bernatchez left Théâtre Repère to work together on various projects of their own. Despite this parting of ways, they remained determined to one day return to the spirit of collective creation that is only possible with an entire theatre troupe.

IN ORBIT FROM ONE THEATRE TO ANOTHER

Now an independent freelancer, the young director from Quebec City began to attract attention. From the National Arts Centre in Ottawa to the Tokyo Globe by way of the Royal Theatre in Stockholm and the Royal National Theatre in London (where he became the first North American to direct a Shakespeare play), major theatres called on Lepage's new vision of dramatic art and his talent as an image maker.

During these travels, Lepage and his team soon noted that each culture has its own approach to theatre and the stage. From one country to another, they had to constantly adapt to different ways of working and to the constraints of each different space. While Lepage notes that the Japanese stand out for their rigour and their respect for the actor's inner life, the Germans have a much more hierarchical approach to the creative process. They expect the director to play the role of an enlightened despot.

Moreover, the process of mounting his works was carried out under sometimes difficult conditions – agents who were efficient but spread too thin, offices (often consisting of only a telephone and a filing cabinet) on three continents, rehearsal halls rented as availability dictated. Without the structure of a real theatre company, the shows were often cobbled together thanks to the support of co-producers and presenters. Flying from one place to another to meet their various commitments, the director and his entourage began to feel the need for a more grounded structure capable of embracing their artistic ambitions.

It was in 1993 when Lepage was directing *Shakespeare's Rapid Eye Movement*, a collage of dreamlike Shakespearean texts created at the Bavarian National Theatre, that the idea of founding a company equipped with its own creative workspace took shape.

A Midsummer Night's Dream
by William Shakespeare.
Royal National Theatre in London.
Photo: Neil Libbert

The Munich experience had been particularly difficult. Lepage and his assistant at the time, Philippe Soldevila, had to deal with an especially fraught production context where the actors performed under duress. By his own admission, it was painful and unpleasant to create under such rigid conditions.

Sketches for the Ex Machina logo by Paquebot Design.
Paquebot Design archives

A HOME AT LAST

Surrounded by a close group of collaborators – actors, designers and producers – Lepage laid the foundations for what would become their company. The spirit behind the project was clear. What was needed was a structure capable of adapting to an organic approach to creating new work. Ex Machina came into being the following year, in 1994.

Weary of having to abide by external conditions imposed by the various companies they worked for, the Ex Machina founders established a basic rule. Companies calling on their services would have to adapt to their working methods. They had travelled the world. Now the world would have to travel to their facilities in Quebec City.

In order to realize its dream, the company required premises suitable for its evolving needs. The space would have to be a laboratory where the company could work free of the constraints of seasonal programming and the pressures of touring. A unique space, it would serve as a crossroads, a meeting point for the performing arts, technology and science. Unlike the premises of most other major theatre companies – such as Ariane Mnouchkine's Cartoucherie in Vincennes and Peter Brook's Bouffes du Nord, which are both creative workshops and performance spaces – the Ex Machina laboratory would be fully dedicated to research and exploration.

Upon hearing that Lepage was looking for a building for his company, Quebec City's mayor Jean-Paul L'Allier proposed an abandoned fire station. It was exactly what the members of the company were seeking. At last they had a home for their projects. They engaged the architects Jacques Plante and Marc Julien (assisted by consultant Michel Gosselin, who had often worked with the company as a musician and stage manager) to design their new premises.

After much reflection on the nature and structure of such a site, in 1997 the Caserne at last became reality. Ex Machina now finally had the means of pursuing its approach and complete freedom to explore an endless variety of creative pursuits.

The main studio during the creation of **Zulu Time**.
Photo: David Leclerc

Top photo:
Fire station No. 5 in 1937. Built in the early 20th century and designed by the architect Georges-Émile Tanguay, the Caserne has a distinctive Second Empire façade.
Photo: City of Quebec archives

Bottom photo:
The Caserne in 2007
Photo: Yves Fillion

The building under renovation in 1996.
Photo: Louise Bilodeau

A Hive of Activity and Experimentation

The Caserne is a multipurpose laboratory devised exclusively for artistic creation. Reflecting the inclinations of its occupants, the space has been designed to encourage exchange and interaction. With activities gravitating around a large studio, the building's layout forces encounters among the various component elements of the company. In order to get to the catwalk to the control room, for example, technicians must go through the administrative offices. Similarly, the windows of the designers' offices look out directly onto the main studio.

Serving as a rehearsal hall for stage performances, a set-building workshop and a film studio, the Caserne is where the company sketches out the first rough drafts, tests hypotheses and gives form and shape to plays before presenting them on stages around the world.

Marie Gignac and Normand Bissonnette in
The Seven Streams of the River Ota.
Photo: Emmanuel Valette

Telling Stories

The personal engages the universal.
The Far Side of the Moon. (Yves Jacques)
Photo: Sophie Grenier

IN LOOKING BEYOND THE IMAGERY AND FORMAL VOCABULARY THAT CHARACTERIZE EX MACHINA PERFORMANCES, WHAT IS IMMEDIATELY APPARENT IS THAT THE DESIRE TO TELL STORIES – FABLES THAT MOVE AND ENGAGE AN AUDIENCE – LIES AT THE VERY HEART OF THE COMPANY'S APPROACH.

In *The Far Side of the Moon*, the main character, Philippe, asks, "How do you reconcile the infinitely banal, the infinitely small, with the infinitely great and the infinitely essential?" This philosophical question is significant to understanding the fabrication of stories at Ex Machina. It is reflected in its performances by a constant dialogue between the personal and the universal, between individual experience and the great movements of human history.

The prologue of *The Far Side of the Moon* announces that this constant to-and-fro between the private and the public, the personal and the planetary, will permeate the play:

> Before Galileo turned his telescope towards its surface, people believed that the moon was a polished mirror, its dark scars and mysterious contours visible reflections of our own mountains and seas.
>
> When much later, in the 20th century, the first Soviet space probe circled the moon and sent back images of its hidden face, the side we can never see, people were astounded to discover that the moon had a second face, one that was much more scored and battered, wounded by countless meteors and storms of celestial debris. Some NASA scientists called it "the disfigured side of the moon." That irony on the part of the Americans, however, was perhaps due to the fact that the prominent features on the dark side of the moon were named after Soviet cosmonauts, poets and inventors.
>
> Tonight's performance is inspired to some extent by the competition between these two peoples, acting as a touchstone for this tale of two brothers, each of whom constantly sees in the other's gaze a mirror reflecting his own wounds and his own vanity.

This unique manner of combining a mundane personal story line with major historical events is omnipresent in the company's plays. Even while they were members of Théâtre Repère and long before founding Ex Machina, Robert Lepage and his associates constructed their fables by constantly shifting between the personal and the universal.

That was very much the case with *Polygraph* (which Lepage created with Marie Brassard in 1988), the story of both a murder and the Berlin Wall. The piece begins with a powerful scene – the autopsy of the victim, which is intermixed with an account of the division of Berlin after the Second World War. Parallels established between the anatomy of the human heart and the functioning of the "wall of shame" compare the valves of the former with the military checkpoints of the latter. This same shifting from minor to major tales can be found in most Ex Machina works. *The Seven Streams of the River Ota* begins in the bombed-out ruins of Hiroshima, while *The Dragons' Trilogy* is based on a few pivotal moments in the history of Canada in the 20th century, including the increased reality of Asian immigration to the country.

Personal stories against a background of historic events.
Evocation of Nazi concentration camps.
The Seven Streams of the River Ota. (Patrick Goyette, Richard Fréchette, Normand Daneau and Éric Bernier)
Photo: Claudel Huot

Individual experience as part of great historical moments.
A soldier in Mao's army in Canton, Sister Marie de la Grâce in Toronto and Charles Bédard riding his bicycle in Quebec City.
The Dragons' Trilogy. Second version.
(Jean-Antoine Charest, Sylvie Cantin and Hugues Frenette)
Photo: Érick Labbé

Cohabitation of seemingly opposite genres.
The naturalism and poetic evocation of **Lipsynch**.
(Left: Hans Piesbergen and Rebecca Blankenship,
Right: Nuria Garcia and Rick Miller)
Photo: Marc Marnie

Photo: Érick Labbé >

CONTEMPORARY MELODRAMA

"Basically, our stories are melodramas!" might seem to be a surprising statement coming from Robert Lepage. Despite the pejorative connotation associated with the term, Lepage persists. "We play with the procedures of melodrama – the omnipresent music, visual effects, the use of stage machinery, the movement of sets. We pull out all the stops when it comes to telling our stories. When you think of it, *The Dragons' Trilogy* is an absolute melodrama. It verges on the pathetic, with its story of the fate of a little girl gambled and lost by her father in a game of cards, a girl who herself gives birth to a little girl who catches meningitis. At the same time, however, the play is transformed and extends beyond its basic issues. After an hour, two hours, three hours, the spectators are fully caught up in the story. They are not only attached to the characters and their melodramatic lives, but they are plunged into the tragedy and the crucial choices that the protagonists must make.

"We like to appeal to the intelligence of the audience. Despite the complexity of the issues and the subject matter, we end up with stories that are relatively simple, or simple at first glance at least. This first level of interpretation allows the spectator to accompany us toward a more universal narrative where the themes reach beyond the scope of the individual's travails. *The Far Side of the Moon* represents the triumph of that idea. People really like the idea that it is a small matter, a family melodrama. But underlying that is history writ large, the major questions of existence, the cosmos, the competition between the Russians and the Americans, the reconciliation between two antagonistic cultures. The subject of the piece is not limited to a fraternal dispute over an inheritance. We broach the matter of reconciliation within the larger framework of the human adventure."

Melodrama

Melodrama is a theatrical genre that was popular in the 19th century. Etymologically speaking, melodrama means drama with music. Following in the tradition of bourgeois drama, its roots are in tragedy, comedy and ritual drama.

Melodrama is characterized by an exaggeration of procedures and an emphasis on acting, directing and staging effects that bolster the moral intrigue, plus a tendency to milk the pathetic elements of the play for maximum effect.

Melodrama
Honoré Daumier
(DR)

The guru Ivanovitch Gurdjieff as viewed by the eye of Olgivanna, the wife of Frank Lloyd Wright. **Geometry of Miracles.** (Rodrigue Proteau)
Photo: Sophie Grenier

A DIALOGUE WITH OTHER DISCIPLINES

From one show to the next, the company has increasingly developed an inclination to explore themes linked to the evolution of thought, and contemporary scientific or artistic issues. As Lepage notes, "We like to create with people who are interested in original ideas, whether in science, technology, philosophy or art. Given our creative process, these preferences end up being reflected in our performances."

In the work of Ex Machina then, the story is constantly interspersed with didactic capsules linked to the theme of the tale. Lepage is particularly interested in the confrontation between thinkers who have had a revolutionary impact on their times and characters whose destiny is more mundane. The director began this staged dialogue with creative genius in *Vinci*, moving on to Jean Cocteau and Miles Davis in *Needles and Opium*, Frank Lloyd Wright and Ivanovitch Gurdjieff in *Geometry of Miracles* and Hans Christian Andersen in *The Andersen Project*.

For Lepage, the notion of accessibility is essential. "When theatre includes ideas from other disciplines, it is important that they be embodied by the characters. Wajdi Mouawad is one of those directors who intelligently manage to integrate new ideas into their work, particularly in *Scorched*. Throughout the play, Jeanne introduces new mathematical theorems that are at the centre of her research. They are interesting, but impossible to understand, until one realizes in a final revelation that Mouawad has been using these equations to build the very structure of his tragedy."

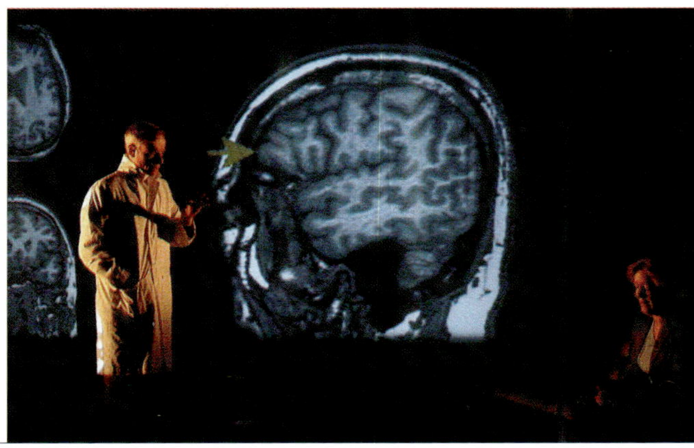

Science is a source of inspiration for Ex Machina. This scene from **Lipsynch** evokes the notions of neurology. (Hans Piesbergen and Frédérike Bédard)
Photo: Jacques Collin

Shaping a Theory in Movement

FROM THE BEGINNING, EX MACHINA HAS METICULOUSLY AVOIDED BEING RESTRICTED TO A SPECIFIC ARTISTIC FRAMEWORK. EACH NEW PIECE IS DEVELOPED USING VARIOUS SOURCES, AND COMPLETE FREEDOM GUIDES THE PROCESS LEADING TO THE FINAL PRESENTATION. AFTER TEN YEARS OF CREATING WORKS AT THE CASERNE, LEPAGE BEGAN TO REALIZE THAT CERTAIN ABIDING FEATURES, OR INDEED RULES, HAD BEEN ESTABLISHED.

Tectonic Plates.
(François Pick and Lorraine Côté)
Photo: Claudel Huot

THEATRE AS EVENT

"Theatre must always be an event." With that notion in mind, Robert Lepage reflects on his approach to theatre. "Everything must contribute to that end. The trap we try to avoid is the logic of the subscription theatre. Far too often, theatres determine their programming based on ticket sales. The question they ask is, 'What do people want to see? What show would please the audience? How should we present it so that it is well received by audiences and critics alike?' In my opinion, that is not the path to take. In aiming to please, one is condemned to duplication. The same ideas are rehashed and served up with the flavour of the day, without taking any risks whatsoever. What is required, in fact, is a diametrically opposite approach. If our plays become must-see events, the audience will show up.

"Why is it that usually I am not interested in sports, yet I'm completely enthralled by the Olympics? It is because that event is about surpassing limits, where the human being is transfigured. During a dive or a sprint, the athletes become more than mortals; they are demigods. We thus encounter the mythical aspect of life. We must aim for the same thing in theatre."

AIM FOR DANGER

"Marc Doré taught us that actors shouldn't try to be number one, but that they should try instead to discover what makes each actor unique. I think that is very important. Don't try to be the best. Show that you are different, and why that difference matters. It always upsets me when I see artists or actors looking for the easiest path to success. To be unique, don't simply repeat what was previously successful. Put yourself in danger; push your limits.

"Similarly, too many people wait to be selected. They are talented, but lack daring. You can't sit back waiting for a theatre or film director to hire you. Artists must speak up, mount their own projects, make themselves irreplaceable. I'm often told, 'It's easy for you, you have substantial resources.' It's true that now we enjoy exceptional circumstances, but in the beginning we had nothing. We didn't wait for someone to call us; we imposed our presence. We are constantly placing ourselves in a position of danger. Obviously, taking risks offers no shield against making mistakes. In creative work, errors are always very instructive. The trick is to learn to turn them to your advantage."

Needles and Opium.
(Robert Lepage)
Photo: Claudel Huot

Elsinore.
(Robert Lepage)
Photo: Emmanuel Valette

THINK OUTSIDE THE BOX

"The solutions to the problems we encounter often lie beyond the universe we have chosen to explore. I learned that lesson at a young age, when I came across a problem of logic in a magazine.

"It's a well-known puzzle, but it was the first time I had seen it. The idea is simple. One must connect the nine dots by making four continuous lines, without ever lifting the pencil from the paper. Like most people who are stumped by this puzzle, no matter what approach I tried there was always one dot that resisted my efforts.

"After thinking about the problem for a moment, I realized that the only way to succeed was to extend the lines beyond the square formed by the nine dots. The solution is disarmingly simple, but my mind prevented me from seeing it. It forced me to remain inside the limits established by the problem. It was a big lesson for me. Always think outside the box.

"The answers to our problems are often found in the most unlikely places. We put up barriers that become insurmountable. If we block ourselves during the creative process, often the best thing to do is to step back and enlarge the sphere of activity.

"That rule is fundamental in the work of Ex Machina. It was by refusing frameworks that we established our approach. We are always seeking to expand our horizons, to test new creative avenues, to commingle ideas and vocabularies, to place ourselves in danger. The company's entire creative process is inspired by that notion."

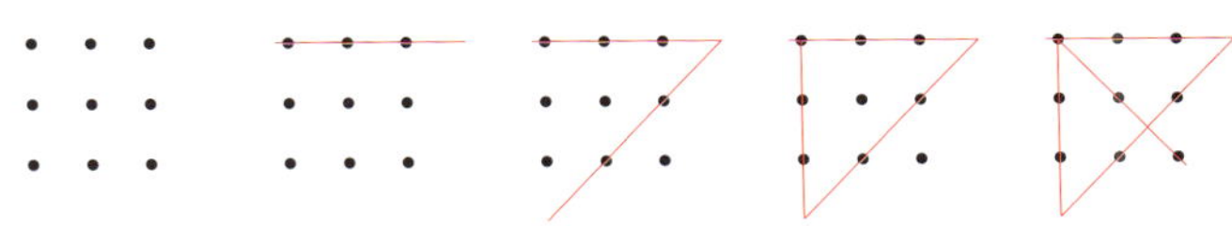

Yves Jacques in **The Andersen Project.**
Photo: Emmanuel Valette

The Creative Process

EXTRACTING FRAGMENTS FROM CHAOS

During the creative process, Robert Lepage often compares the Ex Machina team members to archaeologists – down on their knees in the dirt and equipped with rudimentary tools, they dig, search and unearth the elements of a story.

At the beginning of the excavation it is impossible to predict the results of the search. Layer after layer, piece by piece, the collaborators discover fragments of the narrative. Once the material has been extracted from the earth, it must be cleaned, polished and assembled.

The soil dug up by the Ex Machina researchers is very densely packed with shapes and ideas. Science, technique, history, myths and art all offer opportunities for exploration.

At the outset, anything is possible. The team ventures forward in absolute chaos without benefit of guides or landmarks, with only a few avenues of research acting as beacons. *Needles and Opium*, for example, grew out of a desire to bring together the worlds of Jean Cocteau and Miles Davis by exploring the question of dependency, whether drug addiction or emotional dependency. As for the collective performance *Lipsynch*, it stemmed from a wish to explore the human voice in its myriad manifestations.

Once a trajectory appears to be rich enough for a theatrical project, Robert Lepage invites a few technicians, actors and dramaturges to the Caserne for an initial series of creative workshops. These open-ended brainstorming sessions generate ideas, proposals for concepts and connections. In keeping with the Repère tradition, the participants bring inspirational materials to these sessions: objects, music, brief texts, pictures, books or films, all of which stimulate discussion. The team members recount anecdotes, incidents or dreams inspired by the avenue of research pursued. The importance of these materials becomes relevant only once each individual discloses the personal meaning attached to them. During a *Lipsynch* workshop, the actress and writer Marie Gignac presented a series of silent home movies featuring, among others, her deceased father. In talking about the films, she mentioned that when someone dies without having been recorded, the memory of the person's voice tends to be the first thing to vanish. She could no longer remember the sound of her father's voice, but thanks to the films she had a very precise vision of how he looked and how he walked. That observation became the inspiration for a scene in the play where one of the characters tries to reconstruct the voice of her dead father.

Little by little through the process of accumulation, a universe emerges from the initial chaos, but the dramatic arc of the piece has yet to be determined as the artisans continue to explore all possible avenues. Each path taken and each door opened produce more vivid dramatic materials. Only later will it be assembled in order to construct a narrative.

Table work. **Lipsynch.**
Photo: Jacques Collin

The metaphor of archaeologists is indicative of the state of mind of the participants during the creative phase. "We often have the feeling that the play in its final form exists even before we begin to work," confides Lepage. "It is as though we must invent a way of getting to our destination." That impression brings to mind Michelangelo who, reflecting on his work as a sculptor, noted that "The figure already exits in the block of marble. All that's required is knowing how to set it free."

Paradoxically, for Lepage the idea of a pre-existing play that the artisans must discover does not imply that everything is prearranged. "Each project is to be approached with no preconceived ideas whatsoever. I don't show up at the rehearsal hall thinking, I want to pursue this or that theme in the piece. On the contrary our stories evolve slowly, advancing along with our research, our discoveries and the accidents that occur along the way."

The Dramaturge

In the German theatre tradition, the dramaturge "is the director's scholar as well as his researcher and intellectual advocate." He is the spokesman for the text, a sort of guarantor of meaning. In German theatre the dramaturge is a guide, a literary consultant and an assistant to the director. His work is at the confluence of writing, production and criticism.

At Ex Machina, many individuals have acted as dramaturge in the various productions. They include Peder Bjurman, Adam Nashman and Marie Gignac. To a certain extent, the assistant director Félix Dagenais also plays that role, nourishing the company with his research.

Source: Agnès Pierron, *Dictionnaire de la langue du théâtre: mots et mœurs du théâtre*, Le Robert, 2002, p.187.

Ex Machina projects are carried out simultaneously.
Lipsynch. (Carlos Belda, Sarah Kempt, Lise Castonguay, Rick Miller, Nuria Garcia and Hans Piesbergen)
Photo: Marc Marnie

THE COMPONENT ELEMENTS EMERGE

Unlike the fairly prevalent attitude whereby the artistic and technical dimensions of theatre are two separate entities, Ex Machina is stimulated by dialogue between the component elements of the piece. This approach implies complete openness and receptiveness on the part of the entire team. Since the story emerges from the collective work of the group, everyone – from the technicians to the director – participates in building the piece.

The company is inspired by a certain Brechtian ideal, "where the dramaturgical work is not the privilege of one person or a small group,"[4] albeit as an idealized vision, given that Brecht himself was never able to make that approach work. "At the Berliner Ensemble, Brecht the director composed the fable with the dramaturge, the set designer and sometimes one or two actors. He then made sure that the actors and technicians helped the audience interpret the fable of the play."[5]

For Brecht, the "fable" was analyzed, produced and presented by the entire theatre – actors, set designers, makeup artists, costume designers, musicians and choreographers. All contributed their craft to the joint endeavour, without renouncing their independence.[6] From that proposition, Lepage retained the importance of the component elements of a play. "We often mistakenly believe that theatre is a literary art form. The reason is quite simple. The text or script has long been the only means of preserving any trace of a performance, leaving as a legacy the unwarranted dominance of words over the other component elements, as though the text were of greater value than the rest. At Ex Machina, we believe that all vocabularies contribute to the creation of meaning."

From that particular vision of theatre, Robert Lepage has extracted another rule underlying the Ex Machina creative approach – everything must be done simultaneously. Since all the components contribute to a common objective, it is essential to have them interact so that they all evolve in concert.

The effect of that rule is borne out during all stages of Ex Machina's creation, in which all collaborators are invited to take part. Designers, technicians, actors, the production team, the dramaturge, observers and the director come together starting right at the initial exploratory phase. They are all asked to bring with them inspirational materials to enrich the raw material of the performance.

What is important at this stage is to create a playful ambience conducive to discovery. It is not necessarily a question of creating theatre at this point, but of having fun while exploring various paths. The team makes up games and conducts workshops, the goal being to have the various sections of the play come to the fore without any specific order or desire for plausibility, but as though it involved pieces of a puzzle whose final image remains a mystery.

4. Daniel Couty and others, *Le théâtre*, Paris, Bordas, 1980, p. 149.
5. *Ibid.*, p. 148.
6. Bertolt Brecht, *Petit organon pour le théâtre*, L'Arche, 1999, p. 217.

Objects are transformed into metaphors.
Philippe explores the many possibilities of an ironing board.
The Far Side of the Moon.
(First three photos: Yves Jacques. Last photo: Robert Lepage)
Photos: Ludovic Fouquet

Photo: Jacques Collin

At this stage there are no limits. The actors improvise in all sorts of directions, which leads to the appearance of characters, situations and a rough draft of dialogue. This manner of having the components of the story emerge is reflected later in the very construction of the plays, where a mosaic of meaning emerges from intersecting, interrupted and superimposed dramatic lines.

The initial exercises are not limited to acting. From the outset, much attention is paid to formal research. By manipulating objects, props and set elements, the creative team is able to transform them, spiriting them away from their initial function, giving rise to unexpected metaphors and codes. In *The Far Side of the Moon*, for example, an ironing board becomes a stationary bicycle, an exercise machine and a small child. In *Vinci*, a simple tape measure evokes the pyramids of Cheops, Big Ben, the Great Wall of China, a picture, a camera, a television set and a rifle.

During this time of play, improvisations and workshops, the team also discusses the poetic dimensions of the piece. Choreographic frameworks are established (such as Gurdjieff's tutorial sessions in *Geometry of Miracles* where his disciples imitate his movements), images appear and symbolically charged objects are brought into play (mirrors, syringes, razors, etc.), all of it contributing to the narrative gradually taking shape.

IMPOSING A STRUCTURE ON A WORLD OF POSSIBILITIES

During these initial creative sessions, the team may propose a structure to begin organizing this chaos of infinite possibilities. Often that initial structure is inspired by one or more numbers whose symbolic value or evocative power retains a certain interest. *The Dragons' Trilogy* is a good illustration of that approach. In 1985 during the Canadian tour of *Circulations*, Robert Lepage had the idea of creating a play based on the number 3. It would consist of three parts, and would take place in the three different Chinatowns he had just visited, in three different historical periods. The trilogy would be created in three stages, leading to three different versions of the show (lasting 90 minutes, 3 hours and 6 hours respectively). "That framework allowed for a classical pattern of action, reaction and reconciliation," Lepage explains. "Today we work with much more complex narrative structures. In the cinema, there are several different approaches to script breakdown. Syd Field's analysis of movies divides them into five parts. The Europeans and people like Woody Allen tend to work with a nine-act structure. For *Lipsynch*, we decided to play with that nine-part system, which allowed us to create a much more refined and intriguing structure than we had with *The Dragons' Trilogy*."

Notes for **Elegant Universe,** a play whose theme is the superstring theory of physics. The project was abandoned in 2005.

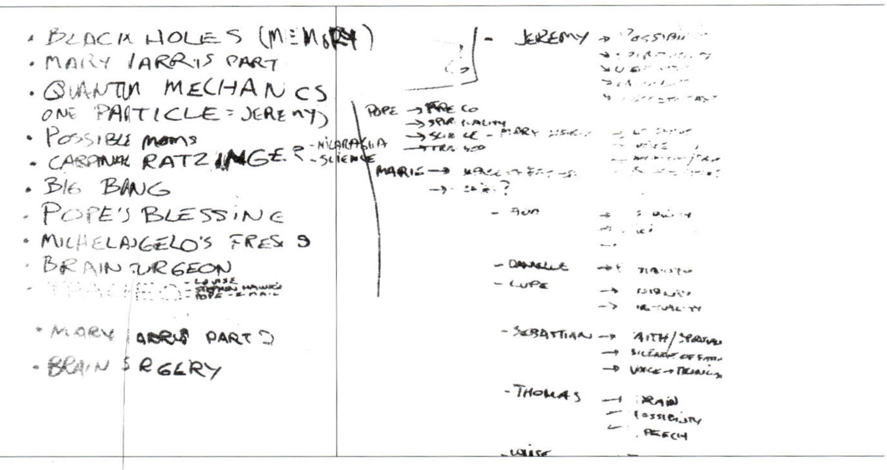

The white board helps in organizing the dramatic paths explored.
The device also provides photocopies of the notes made on its surface.
Photo: David Leclerc

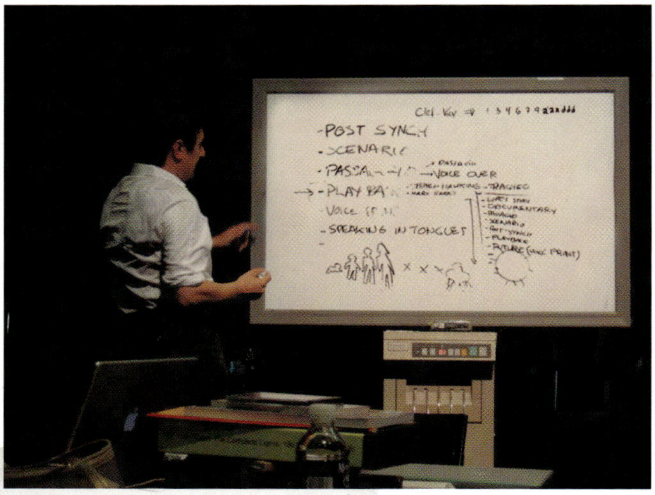

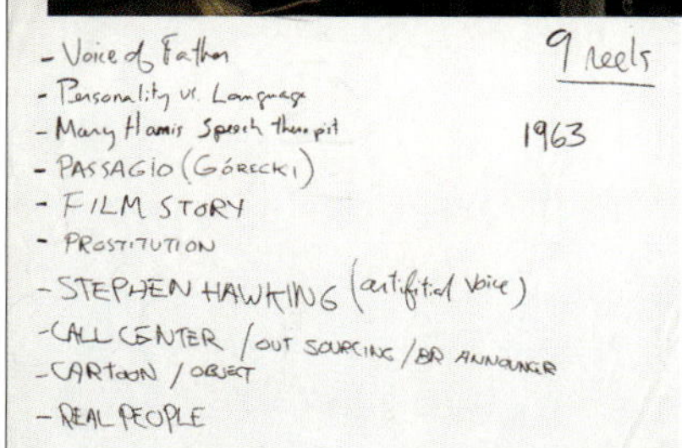

∧ Notes for **Lipsynch.**

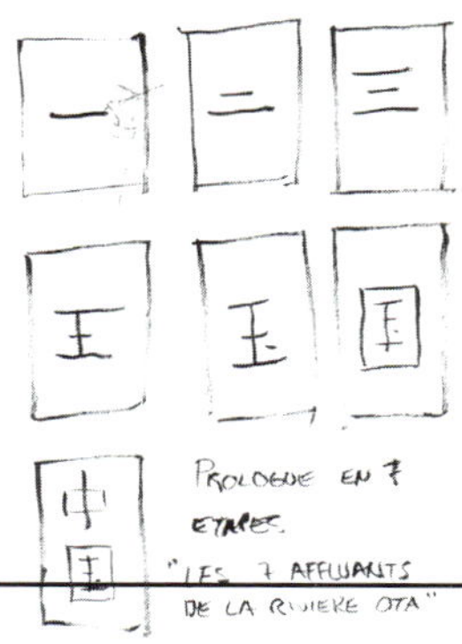

Above and beyond that choice, however, the creators of *Lipsynch* also wanted to develop a flexible dramatic structure. "At first, we were looking to free ourselves from a linear narrative. Rather than opting for the usual route of moving from introduction to conclusion, we were inspired by the architecture of hypertext, a fascinating approach where no order is imposed on the delivery of information. We thus thought of developing nine boxes which were autonomous yet linked. This allowed for a coherent narrative, one that could begin at any one of the boxes. For the moment that hasn't panned out, and we've come to realize that linearity allows for better channelling of the inspiration driving the play. In order for the piece to fall into place, we must maintain control over the phrasing of each scene, the gradation of intentions and the order in which the information is disclosed. Even though this approach has not yet been perfected, it is an interesting avenue to explore in future."

During the course of creating a work, anything can be changed to better serve the story, even the very structure of the tale. That was precisely the case during the creation of *The Seven Streams of the River Ota*. The play was initially divided into twelve parts with the action unfolding in twelve different historical eras over a period of twelve months, in twelve cities located in twelve different time zones.

< Notes for **The Seven Streams of the River Ota.**

The 9-Act Film Structure used for *Lipsynch*

1 – **An event that is not in the film**, but which is necessary for the action of the story to take place. The decision to include this element or not is up to the filmmakers.
2 – **Begin with an image**. The film begins with an evocative image as a prelude to the action.
3 – **Something goes wrong**. Equilibrium is destroyed. The situation must be rectified.
4 – **We meet the hero, and learn of his 3 mishaps.** We see the hero challenged by three events that reveal his character. We don't learn everything, but the audience understands the nature of the hero by a sort of triangulation.
5 – **Commitment.** The hero is committed to rectifying the situation.
6 – **Bad choices.** The hero plunges into action, but for the wrong reasons.
7 – **Reversal.** An event reveals to the hero that he has made a mistake.
8 – **New objective.** New objectives are set. The hero may (or may not) fulfill his task.
9 – **Epilogue.** Resolution of the conflict. The new situation that ensues from this resolution is evoked.

Then the team screened Marguerite Duras' film *Hiroshima, mon amour*. One of the characters in the film mentions the seven streams in the River Ota delta, and thus the number 7 immediately became a reference point for a more organic structure. The importance of that number in Japanese mythology allowed for links to other cultures, particularly Western societies where 7 also plays an important role. As for the division of time, the new approach led to a time frame structured on the seven days of the week.

Once the basic framework has been defined, each section becomes a box containing all the elements created during the exploratory phase. Somewhat like film editors, the collaborators play with extensive blocks of dramatic material, proceeding by trial and error and cut-and-paste before arriving at an arrangement that is the most evocative, the most poetic and the most effective. Bit by bit, the characters' trajectories take shape, thematic groupings occur, elements of set design are clarified and the story seems to tell itself.

Scaffold structure for a techno-cabaret set in airports. **Zulu Time.** (Marco Poulin and Rodrigue Proteau) Photo: Sophie Grenier

CHANCE AND CHAOS

"During the creative process, we try to stay in contact with chaos. Over time we find solutions to problems and choices become clearer. What is to be avoided is remaining stuck in that initial creative profusion of ideas for fear of derailing what we worked hard to assemble. We must try not to take anything for granted, and a good way of doing so is to toy with undermining our systems. When we find something that works we immediately ask, 'What would happen if we did the opposite, if we switched perspectives, if the character wanted something else?' That leads to undreamt-of avenues of research.

"Similarly, we must remain open to chance or happenstance. In the piece we are working on right now, *The Blue Dragon*, one of the characters (Pierre Lamontagne) owns an art gallery. To conduct further research, Marie Michaud visited some gallery owners in Montreal. She wanted to learn how the art market functioned, the relationship between the artists and the galleries, how prices are determined, etc. She met with a few art gallery owners as part of her investigation. Surprisingly enough, each man was named Pierre. It might appear ridiculous, an insignificant coincidence, but we seized on the idea and asked, 'Now why is that? Perhaps it means nothing at all and it won't lead us anywhere. But maybe we're on the right path and we have to dig a little deeper.' During the creative process, many chance occurrences like that appear. They help confirm some of our intuitive choices."

"As I mentioned, our stories are often based on a to-and-fro between the ordinary and the universal. Sometimes, if we pay attention to coincidence, we connect with the grand design of things. In *Zulu Time*, that phenomenon went even further.

"In the beginning, the intention behind the piece was to create an 'airport cabaret' where 26 numbers (for the 26 letters of the international aviation alphabet) would all have a technological component. One week before the events of September 11, we were rehearsing the play before a scheduled presentation in New York. The project had been underway for a few years, yet we kept running up against the same question. Should we develop a story that links all the sequences to each other? Finally, at that point of the process, we decided to do so.

"Starting with the elements that we already had, we began looking for narrative possibilities. After digging and establishing connections, the choices we developed led to the tale of a terrorist bombing aboard an aircraft. The terrorist was a Taliban, and the set consisted of two towers that supported gangways. We had barely begun mounting the show in New York when the events of 9/11 took place. We were stunned by the coincidence! But looking back, it is not such a surprising happenstance. When creating a new work, we develop antennae that pick up anything even remotely linked to our themes. It's often simply a matter of listening to the signals being emitted for our tales to strike a chord."

Robert Lepage: "Opening the door to the warehouse means inviting random chance to become part of the performance. By an extraordinary coincidence, on the night of the premiere a junk sailed by on the St. Lawrence River at the very moment we were performing the scene that takes place in Hong Kong harbour."
The Dragons' Trilogy.
(Richard Fréchette)
Photo: François Truchon

The Actor as Creator – Plunging in Feet First

After working in opera with Robert Lepage, the dramatic soprano Rebecca Blankenship expressed a desire to participate in mounting a new play.
The Seven Streams of the River Ota. (Rebecca Blankenship)
Photo: Claudel Huot

"BASICALLY, JUST WHAT IS ACTING?" ASKS ROBERT LEPAGE. "IT IS TAKING SOMEONE ELSE'S WORDS AND SPEAKING THEM IN SUCH A WAY THAT THE AUDIENCE BELIEVES THAT YOU MADE THEM UP ON THE SPOT. THEATRE ACTING OFTEN MEANS PRETENDING TO DREAM UP WORDS THAT ARE NOT YOURS. THE MORE THE AUDIENCE HAS THE IMPRESSION THAT THE ACTOR HIMSELF WROTE THE WORDS THAT HE IS SPEAKING, THE MORE CREDIBLE HIS PERFORMANCE. SO WHY NOT ASK ACTORS TO WRITE THEIR OWN SPEECHES, TO BECOME PLAYWRIGHTS? I AM INTERESTED IN ACTING ONLY INSOFAR AS IT IS A FORM OF WRITING."

Following in the tradition of Lecoq as transmitted by Marc Doré, this vision of acting is echoed in the company's creative approach. In the search for poetry and stories, at Ex Machina the actor is the raw material.

Selecting those who will be participating in the work is thus of great importance. Ex Machina does not hold auditions, preferring to proceed by invitation. Artists are often chosen following chance encounters. Lepage seeks first and foremost intriguing personalities, people who, through their intuition, their intelligence, their culture, their education and their experience, can provide interesting input to discussions and improvisations.

"Sometimes actors come to me because they want to be involved in a project," explains Lepage. "Often they are experienced artists who feel compelled to write, but by means of their instrument, which is acting. They choose to take a break in their careers as performers and plunge into the adventure of creation."

In his notes, Stanislavski sometimes complained about actors who "come to rehearsals to admire what the director has created."[7] Likewise, Ex Machina has little patience for passivity among its collaborators. Given that the play is built on the contributions of all participants, generosity is a quality highly prized by the company. As Marie Gignac explains, "Actors must not wait to be told what to do. Robert Lepage gives them a lot of leeway. When creating the piece, he gives them very few directions. It is up to the actors to come up with ideas, images and components that will allow the play to move forward."

7. Constantin Stanislavski, *Notes artistiques*, Belfort, Strasbourg, Circé, Théâtre national de Strasbourg, 1997, p. 63.

Over the years Ex Machina has presented several classics. Here Lepage directs Spanish actors in **La Celestina.**
Photo: Érick Labbé

DIRECTING ACTORS

Early in his career, Lepage observed that emotion can often be a trap for actors. A certain acting tradition, promulgated by intellectuals such as Stanislavski, promotes the idea that by internalizing emotions the actor is able to convey those emotions to the spectator. "It is a method that gives excellent results in film – acting that portrays a character's inner world. I am inclined to believe that in theatre, however, that method is full of pitfalls. I realize that there is no automatic relationship between the actor's emotional state and the effect he produces on the audience. That discrepancy is easily measured when a technical problem occurs during the course of the performance. The actor starts to think about the consequences of the problem. Will it happen again? How should he respond? Should he start improvising to play for time? And so on. He is thus no longer in the emotional state of the character. Paradoxically, it is often in those very moments that the actor is most credible. I realized that the actor's role is not necessarily to be personally moved, but to move the audience. There is nothing more self-indulgent than an actor who revels in his own suffering. Internalization is often the wrong tack to take. In order to provoke the desired effect, there is no point in erecting a fourth wall. What is required instead is to convey to the audience the energy of the situation. That means that the emotion must be in the audience, not onstage.

"One way of opening up channels of communication with the audience is by means of humour. In addition to easing acceptance of serious or tragic scenes, laughter has the advantage of allowing the actor to gauge the crowd. *Lipsynch* begins with an extremely harsh scene. Aboard an aircraft, in the first-class section, a soprano is practising an aria while in the last row a child is crying. To me it was interesting to confront the voice in both its full mastery, the voice of the opera singer, and its raw state, the cry of the baby. For now *Lipsynch* starts with the singer Ada starting the first few bars of Henryk Górecki's *Sorrowful Songs*. At the same time, in the rear of the cabin a young woman dies while her baby cries in her lap. The scene lasts fifteen almost unbearable minutes. In the following scene, Ada is on the phone with a Lufthansa agent trying to discover what happened to the child. She has to speak to three different agents before she finds the information she is seeking. To represent the bureaucracy of large corporations, we repeat the scene three times. Each agent is wearing a different jacket, but it is the same actor playing all three. It's vaudeville, but it gets us our first laugh. From that moment on, the actors are reassured. They know that the audience is with them, that they want to see the show."

Middle photo:
Opening scene of **Lipsynch.** (Nuria Garcia)
Photo: Marc Marnie

Ada on the phone with
a Lufthansa agent. **Lipsynch.**
(Rebecca Blankenship and Hans Piesbergen)
Photo: Marc Marnie

Actors sometimes switch characters as a play is being developed. Normand Bissonette originally played the ambassador. He then gave the role to Richard Fréchette in order to play the character of Jeffrey. Similarly, Anne-Marie Cadieux and Macha Limonchik have taken turns playing the role of the actress.
The Seven Streams of the River Ota. The restaurant scene at two different phases of the development process. (Left: Normand Bissonnette, Marie Brassard and Anne-Marie Cadieux. Right: Marie Gignac, Richard Fréchette, Macha Limonchik and Marie Brassard)
Photos: Claudel Huot

READY-TO-WEAR CHARACTERS

In the theatre, actors are often used to being guided. They expect the director to have a precise idea of the play even before rehearsals begin. The actor's task is to merge into a predetermined structure where intentions and gestures are established before rehearsals. At Ex Machina, it is exactly the opposite. The play takes shape according to the rhythm of the discoveries made.
There are no predefined characters at the outset. The actors thus have no idea of what they will be playing. Will an actor have a major role that reflects his status and talent? There is no way of knowing, for he is the person who will be developing characters during improvisations. The company does not hold auditions nor any casting sessions to determine which actors will be in the piece, and age is irrelevant. An actress can play a mother or an ingénue regardless of her actual age.

It is interesting to note that the characters do not belong to those who created them. They belong instead to the story, to the narrative. The fact that an actor develops a role through improvisation does not mean that he will be performing that role. The characters are like costumes – they are ready to wear. They can be loaned, exchanged or given away. Whether it be to move a particular situation forward or to exploit other facets of a character, it is not uncommon to have the actors trade roles along the way.
Similarly, the characters are finally attributed according to the talents of each actor and the demands of the performance. For Lepage, "When transferred from one actor to another, a character is given new life and gains more depth. In the case of solo performances, things unfold differently. When an actor has to replace me, his first tendency is to imitate me. It is only after a certain period of time that he is able to provide his own shading and energy, once he has grasped all the nuances and subtleties of the character."

The Busker's Opera opened up new frontiers for the company. In future, Ex Machina will explore more such encounters of theatre and music.
(Saxophonist and singer Claire Gignac)
Photo: Érick Labbé

COMBINING DISCIPLINES

The contorsionist Jinny Jessica Jacinto. **Zulu Time.**
Photo: Reggie Tucker

From one project to the next, Ex Machina works with artists from many different disciplines. In his desire to break down barriers, Lepage often encourages them to venture beyond their regular forms of expression. Consequently, musicians, dancers and puppeteers often end up acting in company performances. During rehearsals for *The Seven Streams of the River Ota*, the dramatic soprano Rebecca Blankenship (who later appeared in *Lipsynch*) joined the team. *Zulu Time* saw the arrival of the contortionist Jinny Jessica Jacinto, and DJ Killa Jewel (Julie Fainer) contributed her services to *The Busker's Opera*.

Obviously, taking up acting duties demands of the individuals concerned a certain ability to adapt and to let go. Their first appearances are often in response to a temporary need. For example, a secondary character is created during an improvisation and there is no actor available for the role. The non-actors are then asked to perform the character for one rehearsal, a provisional state of affairs that often tends to persist indefinitely.

"I don't have any tricks of the trade to pass on to the actors. I'm not an acting coach. I prefer to stimulate their intelligence, because I realize that actors are more believable when they know what they're talking about."

When directing new actors, Lepage gives them a lot of freedom. The long periods spent working on the show allow them to understand the inherent theatrical dynamics and to make a personal contribution to the ensemble piece. Not all are able to express themselves with ease onstage. Some are less skilled with words, relying more on physical expression. Others manage to find over the course of rehearsal and performance a way of absorbing the theatrical work into their own particular discipline.

In **Geometry of Miracles**, the movement echoes the architecture. Dancers and acrobats are part of the creative team.
Photo: Emmanuel Valette

During the development of **The Seven Streams of the River Ota**, actor Éric Bernier took lessons in butoh dance, sharing what he learned with the rest of the troupe. Here his character does some warm-up exercises.
Photo: Yves Dubé

REPERTOIRE OF MOVEMENT

Apart from words, ideas and characters, the actors at Ex Machina use movement as a form of writing. The company uses explorations of movement to discover sequences of gestures that will serve the story.

Explorations of movement often take place during the warm-up exercises that precede the improvisation sessions. An actor might demonstrate a dance, a kata or a sequence of movements to the rest of the troupe. That becomes a basis for play and variations that will later generate a repertoire of movements that are incorporated into the performance.

The Dragons' Trilogy offers a revealing example of such integration. The troupe was interested in tai chi, a martial art relatively unknown in Quebec at the time. The tao lu sequences (series of tai chi movements) led to the creation of some dreamlike tableaux. "Tai chi also helped in creating narrative codes," explains Lepage. "We discerned in the sequences of movements a close link to specific gestures such as playing cards, smoking opium, washing dishes or offering someone a drink. Starting from those figures, we invented fully-fledged dramatic situations. In that sense, movement made a direct contribution to the writing of the piece."

Sometimes the vocabulary of the body imposes its demands on the set design. For *Needles and Opium*, Lepage used Jean Cocteau's *Lettre aux Américains* as an initial resource. The French writer wrote the letter aboard a flight back home following his first sojourn in the United States. "In his letter, Cocteau took a look at America and at Europe while suspended between two continents, in touch with neither. In order to play Cocteau, I too had to place myself in a state of suspension, so we concocted a set design with a harness that allowed me to leave the ground, to be airborne. As soon as the set was built, I began exploring all sorts of possibilities offered by the harness. Because it opened a door to different ways of moving and playing with perspective, the rigging became a central element in crafting the language of the piece."

Martial arts like kendo provide material for an entire repertoire of movement.
The Seven Streams of the River Ota. (Normand Daneau)
Photo: Claudel Huot

Ex Machina and Dance

Dance increasingly plays a significant role in the work of Ex Machina. For *The Geometry of Miracles* (where connections were established between mathematics, architecture and the human body), Lepage invited some dancers to join the actors in the creative process. The piece called for a particular physicality, an embodiment of abstract ideas. To achieve that goal, the team integrated Gurdjieff's dances and Meyerhold movement sequences into the performance.

This combination of dance and theatre is currently being pursued in the show that Robert Lepage is developing with the dancer Sylvie Guillem. The project (working title *Eonnagata*) is based on the historical figure of the knight Éon and makes use of onnagata codes. In the Noh and Kabuki theatrical traditions, onnagata is a man who performs a role that symbolizes femininity.

Dancer Sylvie Guillem and choreographer Russell Maliphant explore a movement sequence. **Eonnagata.**
Photos: Gilles Tapie

Sequence of movements created by Vsevolod Meyerhold. **Geometry of Miracles.** (Thaddeus Philipps, Tea Alagic, Marie Brassard, Rodrigue Proteau, Denis Gaudreault, Jean-François Blanchard, Anthony Howell, Daniel Belanger and Catherine Tardif)
Photo: Ex Machina archives

Suspended upside down, the dancers perform an aerial tango.
Zulu Time. (Claire Gignac and Rodrigue Proteau)
Photo: Reggie Tucker

Left:
The Andersen Project.
(Robert Lepage)
Photo: Érick Labbé

Right:
The Far Side of the Moon.
(Robert Lepage)
Photo: Emmanuel Valette

MOUNTING SOLO SHOWS

As Lepage notes, "the solo show involves choosing one of three forms of communication – an interior monologue, a conversation with the audience or a dialogue with an offstage character. I generally prefer the third option, because it provides more freedom and allows for integration of the other two forms." To give substance to this dramatic choice, Lepage had to develop a repertoire of subterfuges that would allow him to suggest the presence of other characters: telephone conversations, gestures that foreshadow subsequent communication (sending an e-mail, filming a home movie), or using objects connected to other characters (a leash attached to the neck of an invisible dog, for example).

In starting work on a solo performance, Lepage needs to take a step back in order to have an overview of the piece being constructed. He employs an understudy or stand-in, an actor who will temporarily play the roles that the director will perform later on. By means of this "shadow," Lepage is able to visualize the performance space and understand the obstacles and possibilities of the set design gradually taking shape. He directs the preliminary explorations of the shadow before eventually taking over the role himself. His stand-in remains on call, however, so that the director is able at any time to step back from the action and cast a critical eye on the proceedings.

Needles and Opium.
(Robert Lepage)
Photo: Ex Machina archives

The collaboration of the dramaturge is also invaluable in the writing of solo pieces, providing resources and approaches that nourish the process, and that also offer Lepage certain acting choices.

During performances, the shadow performs diverse stage business and, on occasion, literally takes Lepage's place during costume changes so that the rhythm and fluidity of the show are maintained.

The Andersen Project >

Normand Poirier, the understudy in **The Andersen Project,** waltzes with a mannequin in the Odense scene.
Photo: Félix Dagenais

The stand-in allows the director to visualize the performance space.
The Andersen Project.
(Robert Lepage and Normand Poirier)
Photo: Félix Dagenais

In improvisation, the stand-in becomes "the other person," allowing for development of situations where Lepage is talking to an offstage character.
The Andersen Project.
(Normand Poirier and Robert Lepage)
Photo: Jean Lebourdais

With the understudy onstage, the director can view proposed videos from the house.
The Andersen Project.
(Normand Poirier)
Photo: Jean Lebourdais

Confrontation between Beelzebub and Frank Lloyd Wright in the desert. **Geometry of Miracles.**
(Tony Guilfoyle and Rodrigue Proteau)
Photo: Emmanuel Valette

A New Theatrical Language

Robert Lepage and his collaborators have courageously embarked on a vast and utterly necessary endeavour. They seek to create theatre where the terrifying, incomprehensible reality of our contemporary era and the small, insignificant yet very important details of our daily lives are expressed by means of theatrical language where technology is used to serve and support human beings. Quite the task! What a splendid ambition![8] Peter Brook

At the opening of the Vieux Colombier theatre in Paris in 1913, Jacques Copeau published a manifesto proclaiming that dramatic truth is revealed in actions and feelings, to the exclusion of other theatrical elements, which he dismissed as mere decoration.
"To be fascinated by the inventions of engineers or electricians is to grant to a painting, a stage backdrop or the lighting design undeserved prominence. It is to succumb to trickery and effect. Old or new, we renounce them all. Good or bad, rudimentary or sophisticated, real or artificial, we intend to deny the importance of stage machinery. The constraints of the stage and its base artifice will serve as discipline, forcing us to concentrate all truth in the feelings and actions of our characters. Let other glories disappear. For the new theatre, just give us a bare stage![9]

Integrating video as a narrative device.
The Busker's Opera. (Julie Fainer and Marco Poulin)
Photo: Érick Labbé

Installed in the centre of the performance space, the stage forms a set where high tech and low tech meet.
Zulu Time. (Claire Gignac, Diane Labrosse, Jinny Jessica Jacinto, Michel F. Côté and Marco Poulin)
Photo: Emmanuel Valette

8. Peter Brook, *Un travail mal compris*, letter to the editor published in *Le Devoir*, Saturday, May 25, 1996, p. A10.
9. Jacques Copeau, *Un essai de rénovation dramatique*, in *Registre 1, Appels*, Gallimard, 1974, p. 37.

Describing a rape scene. Video allows for a certain distancing.
Lipsynch. (Nuria Garcia)
Photo: Érick Labbé

Without repudiating the heritage of Copeau nor the potential of the bare stage, Robert Lepage sees in the clash of the component elements of a play an opportunity to generate new ideas, images and forms of speech and, eventually, new narratives.

This approach leads to a constant dialogue between form and content. Many commentators, however, see in the work of Ex Machina merely a formal exercise. Lepage challenges that interpretation: "Our main intention is to tell a story, not to construct captivating images or indulge in razzle-dazzle. Unlike some others, we do not limit ourselves in the ways and means deployed to tell the story. Often when presenting the great works of the repertoire, artists seek the best way of illustrating the existing text. We, however, rely on an extensive repertoire of theatrical tools, where the script is but one resource among many. According to that approach, the actors, as well as the designers and the technicians, become playwrights."

Robert Lepage often compares his role to that of a traffic cop. "We soon end up with a phenomenal quantity of approaches, ideas, images and resources. My first task is to control the circulation of ideas and information. I do not seek to impose my vision, but rather to create fertile ground so that video, costumes, music, set design and all the other component elements can exist in harmony and be mutually inspiring."

In that regard, Lepage's position is similar to Brecht's take on the role of the director. "The director does not come into our theatre with his idea or his vision, or a preconceived plan for blocking and set design. His desire is not to realize his concept. His duty is to stimulate and organize the productive work of the actors, painters, musicians, etc."[10]

"In fact," continues Lepage, "the work is driven by the project. Initially, I wanted *The Blue Dragon* to be a solo show. I quickly realized that the piece would require two actors. We have now come to the conclusion that it calls for three actors. It's the same thing for the other component elements. Some pieces require the presence of a musician performing live onstage. Others, like *Lipsynch*, call for all the technological elements – video, sound, technicians – being visible onstage, accompanying the actors. Regardless of our intentions, solutions arise as the various elements of the production take form. That brings us to another rule that applies to our work. We must be attuned to the performance. The path pursued is dictated by the play, not by the director."

10. Bertolt Brecht, *Journals: 1934-1955*, New York, Routledge, p. 146.

A MORE DYNAMIC NARRATIVE UNIVERSE

By mingling the recording arts and the performing arts, Ex Machina constantly aims to reinvent its narrative codes. When he suggested that musician and composer Bernard Bonnier set up his instruments onstage during presentations of *Circulations* in 1984, Lepage gave the first indications of his distinctive signature, marked by a multidisciplinary approach to staging. He has repeated the experience with the composers Robert Caux (*The Dragons' Trilogy*, *Needles and Opium*, *Elsinore*) and Michel F. Côté (*The Seven Streams of the River Ota* and *Zulu Time*).

The composer and arranger Jean-Sébastien Côté (who has been working with the company since *The Far Side of the Moon*) describes some of the demands of the situation: "The first thing is to propose music and solutions to problems that arise, but it is also important to know how to respond to the unexpected. As we never know where the work will lead us, it's always best to keep an ace up your sleeve. I make sure I have some music and effects in reserve in order to respond to unforeseen demands."

LOW TECH/HIGH TECH

From one project to another, Ex Machina has expanded opportunities for a dialogue between theatre and technology. Whether it be by means of music, video, lighting or set design, the company always tries to make maximum use of the possibilities of cutting-edge technology. "An abiding feature of our work," says Michel Bernatchez, "is that in our shows there is always a sort of confrontation – or cohabitation – between high tech and low tech. We work with advanced technologies, but the presence of extremely simple elements provides a counterbalance." *The Andersen Project* illustrates that characteristic. The show makes use of certain complex technologies such as a flexible screen that offers, as needed, a concave or convex projection surface, or dynamic video masking. But in this complex universe, one of the most striking scenes involves pantomime shadow theatre to illustrate one of Andersen's stories, *The Shadow*. Holding a simple lamp, the performer produces a series of images on a large screen. "I suppose that the encounter between high tech and low tech opens the way to a certain poetry. If it were simply a demonstration of sophisticated techniques, we would be confined to an impressive but cold universe," concludes Bernatchez.

Ex Machina – An R&D Lab

During the creative process, the artisans at Ex Machina are often confronted with the limits of existing technologies. The company then has to develop innovative solutions in response to the artistic demands of the creative team. At the Caserne, Ex Machina has a research and development department devoted to stage technologies.

It was in this laboratory (under the direction of Tobie Horswill and Catherine Guay) that the company developed, among other inventions, dynamic video masking that takes the performer's silhouette and projects it onto a screen. Conversely, the system can project the video everywhere onstage except on the performer. The applications of this research are now used in other company shows, particularly in operas.

Other performing arts companies are often interested in products developed at the Caserne. That is the case with *Élipsis*, an inter-lens shutter for a video projector lens that allows for a total "video blackout" onstage (an important tool for performances with copious projections of imagery). The shutter has been on the market for the past several years.

The shadow count appears.
The Andersen Project. (Yves Jacques)
Photo: Emmanuel Valette

Technology as a character in the narrative. Robot ballet designed by Bill Vorn and Louis-Philippe Demers. **Zulu Time.**
Photo: Emmanuel Valette

Inviting Observers to the Caserne

Allowing observers into the Caserne is important for Ex Machina. At each stage of the creative process, the company invites researchers, artists and actors interested in learning more about its working methods. In many cases this is mutually beneficial. The creative team benefits from the original viewpoints of observers (who often come from other countries) regarding the work underway. Conversely, the observers learn about the singular creative approach of Ex Machina. Likewise, the company's archives and documentation centre is accessible to researchers and students from both here and abroad. The Caserne also offers guided tours of the premises.

Behind the Scenes

BREAKING DOWN HIERARCHIES

There is a fairly common trend in the Western theatre tradition toward the hierarchical division of theatrical labour. Enthroned at the top of the pyramid are the director and the artistic director. On the next level down are the actors, selected during auditions. Then come the designers, who are often perceived as liaisons between the artistic and technical aspects of the production. At the bottom level are the technicians, who are often the last to be invited to take part. This results in fairly conspicuous control by the "higher" positions over the rest of the production.

In fact, everyone involved in the performance contributes to the success of the ensemble piece. In any show, a stagehand or a lighting or sound technician is obliged sooner or later to develop creative solutions to practical problems that arise. Each individual thus influences the artistic content of the play. When he was working in Tokyo, Robert Lepage was impressed by the relations among the different trades. "In Japan there is an acute awareness of the fact that the visible aspect of a play – that of the actors, the director and the designers – cannot exist without its counterpart in the wings, in the flies, in the control booth and in the offices. It is what they call the flip side of the performance."

Due to the technical complexity of Ex Machina productions (and also for philosophical reasons), the company tends to distance itself from the Western model. The play is approached as an organic entity, an attitude that Lepage summarizes with the comment, "Hierarchies must be done away with."

Each person working on a piece has a certain overview of the project. For example, the technicians not only carry out their traditional duties of ensuring the smooth functioning of the stage equipment and machinery, but are also very much involved in the creative process.

As Lepage notes, "Our technicians have a paradoxical role. They must integrate technical aspects into a poetic universe. We do not expect them to be artists, but they must have an artistic sensibility. As a show is being created, they are constantly called on to come up with solutions. The video technician, for example, must find ways to produce camera and image processing effects. To do so, he must understand not only the technical aspects of his work, but also the underlying poetic inspiration of the piece."

In **Lipsynch,** choreographing set changes requires close collaboration between actors and technicians. (Rebecca Blankenship)
Photo: Érick Labbé

MAKING THE PLAY POSSIBLE

Lipsynch illustrates the importance of this aspect. In addition to their regular duties, the technicians are literally integrated into the dramatic structure of the play. "During a public rehearsal of the play at the Caserne, we noticed that the many set changes and the physical limitations of the space meant that the technicians were constantly onstage or in contact with the actors. Our initial intention was to 'polish' the performance so that the backstage mechanics would become invisible, but the spectators at the rehearsal advised against it. In their opinion, unveiling what goes on backstage – the technicians rolling up extension cords, moving cases and equipment, operating instrument consoles – reflected the theme of the piece. It was an ideal opportunity. The subject of *Lipsynch* is the human voice in all its manifestations, which of course implies an interest in recording techniques such as dubbing and post-synchronization. Their response meant that we could perform entire scenes with the control booth visible onstage. Suddenly the stage technicians became onstage technicians. Not only did we do away with hierarchies during the creative process, but the theme of the piece provided us with the pretext to do the same thing during performances."

It is sometimes said of the production team at Ex Machina that it lays down the rails just ahead of the advancing locomotive. It is a fitting image. The creative machine advances at a frenetic pace while the production team prepares the ground ahead, attending to all sorts of details. From planning future productions to coordinating tours and soliciting foreign presenters and co-producers, the production team is responsible for a wide range of company activities. If, as Lepage says, "the project dictates the direction to take," it also determines certain modes of production. While leaving as much liberty as possible to the creative team, the company must devise technical approaches that are in harmony with the artistic work. The main feature is of course flexibility, which comes in handy when plunging into a project with no preconceived ideas of the final form it will take.

As is the case with most theatre companies, the production team also plays an artistic role at Ex Machina. Their participation mirrors the collaborative relationship between Robert Lepage and Michel Bernatchez, which dates back to the days of the director's first projects. "Over the years," says Lepage, "our professional relationship has become the sort of close collaboration one sometimes sees in cinema between the director and the producer. By giving the director the means to create, the producer influences and shepherds the work. Our approach is quite similar. Michel Bernatchez closely monitors the evolution of each piece. His team – particularly Louise Roussel, the production manager for many of our shows since *The Seven Streams of the River Ota* – gives us the tools we need, while influencing our artistic choices with their comments."

TAKING ADVANTAGE OF CONSTRAINTS

Over the course of the process leading to the performance, the lack of resources sometimes obliges the creators to find unforeseen solutions to practical problems. "When mounting *The Dragons' Trilogy*, we built the show around items and props purchased in thrift shops in the St. Roch neighbourhood," recalls Michel Bernatchez. "With a few suitcases, some old shoes and a parking attendant's booth, Lepage and his team managed to create a comprehensive, cohesive universe. I still say today that brilliant ideas often crop up when you're trying to overcome constraints."

A TREASURE-TROVE OF CAST-OFF MATERIAL

This approach to creating a play, which consists of generating the greatest quantity of material possible in terms of both form and content, eventually imposes a need for radical choices on the part of the creative team, with many good ideas inevitably cast aside. *The Seven Streams of the River Ota* is the play that best illustrates this characteristic. During the three years of developing the project, the 7.5-hour performance was cut by three hours. For each hour of the final version presented in Montreal, Australia and New Zealand in 1997, one hour of material created onstage during one or more of the public rehearsals disappeared over the course of rewrites. Lepage has noted over the years that the company has become more serene about material that is developed only to be cut later on. In fact, not all of the discarded material is lost, for some comes back to earth and resurfaces in another project.

The hackney coach scene allowed for an exploration of Hans Christian Andersen's fascination with eroticism and travel. The upper half of the body is dressed as Andersen, while the lower half represents a young prostitute in a brothel in Paris. Despite its artistic qualities, the scene was eventually cut. Lepage felt that it revealed facets of the character that were best left mysterious. **The Andersen Project.** (Robert Lepage)
Photos: Erick Labbé

Assembling the set for **The Far Side of the Moon** at the Moscow Chekhov Art Theatre. (Robert Lepage)
Photo: Jean-Sébastien Côté

ESTABLISHING THE MEANS TO CREATE

The scope and technical complexity of the Ex Machina projects mean that the issue of human and material resources is closely linked to the company's artistic production, and imaginative solutions are required for financing. Over the years, Michel Bernatchez and Jean-Pierre Vézina, the company vice-president in charge of finance, have established a production structure that provides the creative team as much as possible with the means to fulfil their ambitions. Generally speaking, Ex Machina divides its projects into two categories: creative projects on the one hand, and commissioned projects (operas, museum exhibits, events, etc.) on the other. The company is a rarity in the performing arts milieu in that it has a network of international partners who often contribute financially to its creative projects even before work gets underway. Each project involves an average of some fifteen producers, European theatres and festivals for the most part. In return, Ex Machina guarantees them performances at their venues.

Since the company is firmly committed to international presentations, it engages booking agents as its representatives virtually all over the world. Their role consists mainly of acting as intermediaries with co-producers and selling the company's shows. Ex Machina is currently represented by three agents: the Paris agent is responsible for Europe (excluding Great Britain and Ireland) and Japan; the London agent covers England, Ireland and Scotland; while the Montreal agent is responsible for North and South America, Australia and New Zealand plus Asia, except for Japan.

Allowing for Risk

The fact that Ex Machina's main focus is the international market entails a certain amount of risk. On an annual budget of almost $10 million, the majority of the company's independent revenue (more than 80%) is generated in foreign currency (mainly in euros), while more than 80% of Ex Machina's expenditures are made in Quebec in Canadian dollars. As Jean-Pierre Vézina explains, "contracts are often signed many years before payment. We are consequently susceptible to currency fluctuations. I would not want to have to announce to the company that $100,000 has been cut from a project because of a devaluation of the euro." To avoid that sort of situation, the company adapts to financial markets by opting for coverage in the form of currency risk hedging, whereby a fixed rate of exchange is established for its revenues.

A Timeframe Conducive to Creating

IN ORDER TO HAVE THE TIME FOR IDEAS TO FORM AND TAKE ROOT, EX MACHINA DEVELOPS ITS WORKS IN SEVERAL STAGES. THE DURATION OF EACH CREATIVE PERIOD VARIES FROM ONE TO SEVERAL WEEKS, DEPENDING ON THE PROJECT AND ITS STAGE OF DEVELOPMENT.

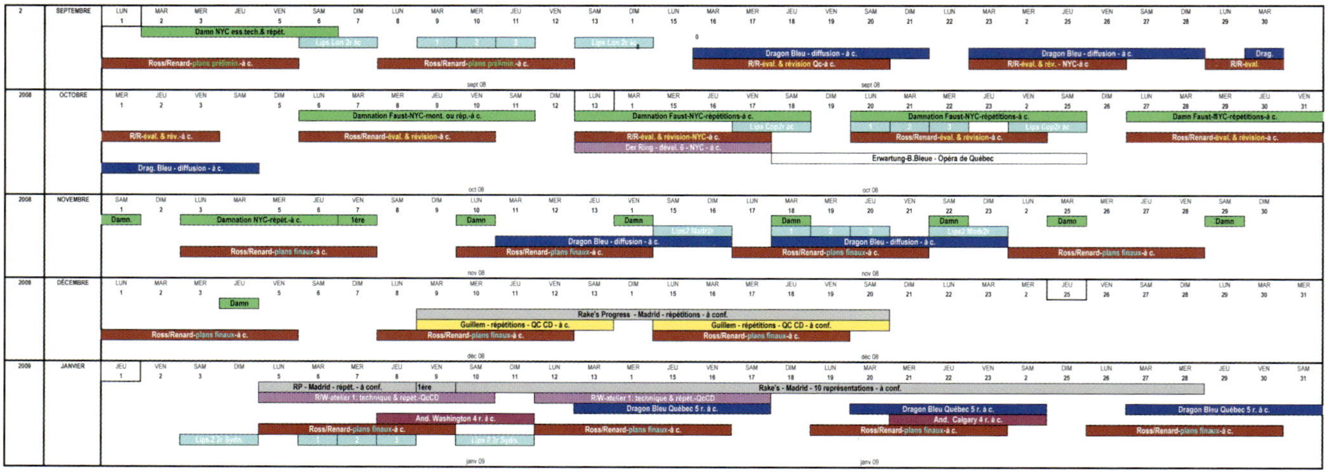

The scheduling of tours, upcoming projects and development periods can be a complex task.
Timetable of present and future Ex Machina productions as of September 25, 2007.

Generally speaking, conventional theatres are subject to predetermined timeframes for mounting a play. First comes a few weeks of rehearsal to explore the nuances of the script and block out the stage action. In French theatre in Quebec, this period usually lasts from six to eight weeks. Then the team moves into the performance space where the set is mounted, the lights hung and sound levels adjusted. The actors have only a few days to adapt to the physical environment of the theatre before performing before an audience on opening night. This method has its advantages, but does not offer the possibility of stepping back to take stock and reflect. From the first day of rehearsal, the team plunges into a one-way tunnel heading straight to the final performance.

The artisans at Ex Machina, however, prefer working concurrently on several projects that are at different stages of development. This approach was originally adopted to accommodate the busy schedules of Robert Lepage and a few other company collaborators. It was difficult to spend more than a few weeks on a project when another production required urgent attention.

Over time, this constraint has become an advantage. At the end of the initial creative process, the team has the leisure of disconnecting from the project and letting the dust settle. In almost unconscious fashion, however, the work continues – images take shape, connections are established and solutions to problems appear.

The audience consists of individuals close to the company and people interested in its artistic approach.
Photo: Jacques Collin

Public rehearsal of **Lipsynch** at the Caserne.
Photo: Érick Labbé

Public rehearsals also generate feedback from other artists on how the work is progressing. Here Robert Lepage discusses a project with Peter Brook.
Photo: Bengt Wanselius

At the start of the next phase of the play's development, team members expound on their most recent ideas before resuming work that will lead to the finished piece. Once again, this is an organic approach. Each project has its own rhythm, and the time allocated to creating the piece is not determined in advance. From "table work" to improvisation sessions and rehearsals, the incubation process can stretch from six months to several years, with collective projects obviously taking more time. *The Seven Streams of the River Ota* was created in approximately five months spread out over a three-year period. As there are fewer collaborators involved in the solo projects, the creative process is relatively shorter. Even in that case, however, it takes place over several sessions spaced out over a lengthy timeframe.

A DAY AT THE CASERNE

The daily work schedule is determined by an organization of time based on the needs of the project. A typical day is divided into three parts that involve designers, technicians, actors, production personnel and observers.

The team meets at 9 a.m. to improvise and rehearse, with everyone suggesting new paths worth exploring or new areas of research. This morning session also allows for an inventory of the props and set elements required for further explorations. The main hall is taken over in the afternoon by the designers and technicians who, one after the other and according to the project demands, settle on bits of music, install a camera in the set, make adjustments to the lighting or build props in the Caserne workshops. At the same time, the assistant director, the actors and the observers conduct research in response to questions or to needs made apparent during the morning session.

In the evening everyone resumes the work begun that morning. The actors and designers can thus test, that very day onstage, the approaches and ideas proposed a few hours earlier.

If the play's progress allows, on Saturday there is a run-through of all the scenes worked on during the week. This initial presentation provides a rough idea of how all the scenes developed in the previous few days fit together.

PUBLIC REHEARSALS

During the creative process, the team feels the need for a verification of various hypotheses, an opportunity to validate certain intuitions. To that end, Ex Machina presents public rehearsals. During this initial contact with outside observers, the audience consists of people close to the company and individuals interested in its artistic approach. It is a first test, revealing what works and what does not. This encounter with an audience is not an ordinary rehearsal – it is a full run-through of the play in its existing state. Making the space and the story ready for visitors involves a certain risk, as the team must find solutions (often temporary) to technical problems, establish transitions between scenes and endeavour to make the piece come together as a whole. The public rehearsal thus serves as another catalyst for the creative process.

It is also an opportunity to discover some of the inherent problems, which often appear in layers. Generally technical matters – moving sets, making lighting adjustments, problems with the stage machinery – are dealt with first. Once they have been resolved, the performance takes on a more fluid rhythm. The focus can then shift to dramatic problems – implausibility, overlong passages, redundancies, etc. In return for admission to the public rehearsal, the spectators agree to provide feedback. Since the creation of *Lipsynch*, Ex Machina has made an e-mail address available for spectators' comments and impressions. During the development phase that follows the public rehearsal, the team begins by reading all comments received. This is particularly useful information for the artisans, as these are generally the first outside opinions they have received about the project.

A PERFORMANCE IS BORN

In theatrical institutions like the Théâtre du Nouveau Monde in Montreal, the Odéon in Paris or the National Theatre in London, various production, programming or marketing demands impose the need for a presentation of a definitive version of the play on opening night. From the first raising of the curtain to the final presentation of the run, the spectators see performances that are practically identical – the same story is told, in the same order and with the same transitions. The first performance becomes fixed and definitive, final, something that can be reproduced.

At Ex Machina, the first performance is considered the start of the second writing phase. While the foregoing periods of exploration and rehearsal have helped define the structure and the ingredients of the narrative, the presence of an audience indicates what works and what does not. Performing to spectators obliges the troupe to focus on efficiency and coherence. The writing process thus continues while the show tours. "Time is one of the important elements in the Ex Machina working method," explains Lepage. "Time passes and things evolve. A bad performance will at least have allowed us to explore, to advance. The longevity of our shows provides us with the chance to construct, to deconstruct and to reconstruct the plays in order to find the best dramatic arc possible."

Lepage often travels to a production the day before a series of performances in order to rework entire sections of the show. Every time, the team is on tenterhooks. What will be changed? Will the transitions take place smoothly? Will the technical crew be able to adapt? The risks are sometimes substantial, but are an integral part of the Ex Machina process. In some cases, the exercise is indeed perilous. The original version of *The Andersen Project* in Quebec City lasted 2 hours and 40 minutes with no intermission. The director was well aware that the piece had some overlong passages but did not have the perspective to step back and make the necessary cuts. During a subsequent tour, Lepage decided to completely rewrite the show over the course of a few days, cutting some forty minutes of material.

To give a more dynamic rhythm to the piece, the order of the scenes was completely revised. In the process Lepage also added a new tale, *The Shadow*, and two new improvised scenes. "On the afternoon of the premiere, I was talking to Michel Bernatchez and Marie Gignac about two scenes that we had had no time to prepare. I explained what I wanted to do in the scenes, what I wanted to say. Bernatchez suggested I take the plunge. Since I had all the elements at hand, it was time to test them before an audience. Just before going onstage I prepared a sort of plan, a list of my ideas, and then I improvised on those ideas. It was creation on the fly! Fortunately we work with nets. Given our working method, we create an enormous amount of material, so we can easily draw on that material in time of need."

THE REPERTOIRE

In recent years Ex Machina has been building a repertoire, which will allow the company to indefinitely present the major plays it has developed since its founding. Two years ago it also started systematically publishing its play scripts. A fairly banal gesture, perhaps, but one that marks the outcome of a long process. Putting something on paper is, in principle, the final step in the evolution of the company's projects. Then again, the publication of scripts sometimes gives new life to a production. On the one hand, the plays can now be presented by other companies (*Polygraph*, for example, has been presented by Italian, Spanish and Japanese theatres) and, on the other hand, students, researchers and fans now have access to the Ex Machina universe by means of these books.

Le Diamant

Ex Machina's desire to establish a repertoire of its works logically implies the idea of a permanent performance space in Quebec City as a site to present its plays.

Before leaving public life, Quebec City mayor Jean-Paul L'Allier invited many cultural organizations to submit proposals for the revitalization of an abandoned highway tunnel that had been dug into the Cap Diamant cliff. A few years later, in 2007, Ex Machina proposed the installation of a performance space in the tunnel to be named Le Diamant.

More than a theatre or playhouse, the Diamant will be an extension of the artistic incubator that is the Caserne. It will provide Ex Machina with the chance to establish a permanent troupe performing its repertoire. It will also allow for revisions of recent shows while the company is on hiatus from its touring obligations. Two major cultural institutions in Quebec City have become partners in the Diamant project, which will become a permanent performance home for them – the Gros Becs theatre for young audiences, and the Carrefour international de theatre festival. Theoretically, the site could include two performance spaces that would allow the three organizations involved to present to Quebec City audiences top-tier plays, both local and international.

The tunnel that will be home to Le Diamant.
Photo: City of Quebec

An Eternal Quest – In Search of the Other

Since its inception, Ex Machina has been adapting its working methods to its evolving artistic ambitions. The task of creating this book obliged us to sketch a portrait that is fixed, if not frozen, in time – a snapshot of the company at a specific moment in its history – that unfortunately does not do justice to the effervescent, ephemeral and ever-changing nature of its approach.

During the course of writing this book, the artisans of Ex Machina reflected on the challenges they hope to take up in the years to come. These include performing for audiences in increasingly accessible countries like China, Russia and India, places where the company has so far done very little touring. For Ex Machina, the shock of encounters with cultures rich in strong theatrical traditions will no doubt provoke hybrids and fusions that will be transformed in turn into new approaches to staging. Works in development such as *The Blue Dragon* are nourished by such dialogue with cultures that now seem much less foreign.

The scene featuring the torii (gateway of a Shinto temple) in Hiroshima.
The Seven Streams of the River Ota. (Éric Bernier and Ghislaine Vincent)
Photo: Jacques Collin

FIELD NOTES, *THE BLUE DRAGON* PROJECT JUNE 2007

MONDAY, JUNE 18
TUESDAY, JUNE 19
WEDNESDAY, JUNE 20
THURSDAY, JUNE 21
FRIDAY, JUNE 22
SATURDAY, JUNE 23

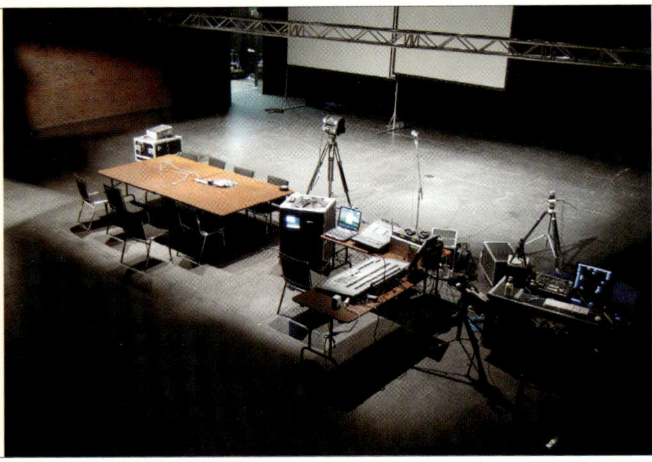

The Caserne. Studio 1.
Montage for **The Blue Dragon.**
Photo: David Leclerc

DURING THE WRITING OF THIS BOOK, EX MACHINA CONDUCTED A WORKSHOP OF *THE BLUE DRAGON*, A PLAY SCHEDULED TO OPEN A FEW MONTHS LATER, IN SPRING 2008. A LOG WAS KEPT AS A MEANS OF SHEDDING LIGHT ON THE CHOICES, DOUBTS, PROBLEMS AND DISCOVERIES THAT ARE A PART OF DAILY LIFE AT THE COMPANY.

MONDAY, JUNE 18

Morning Work Session

The week began with a production meeting led by Robert Lepage. Attending the meeting were Michel Bernatchez (producer), Julie-Marie Bourgeois (production manager for the project), Félix Dagenais (assistant director), Marie Michaud (actor), Michel Gauthier (set designer), David Leclerc (videographer), Christian Garon (stage manager), Pierre Gagné (stagehand), and Patrick Caux (one of the authors of this book).

The meeting began with a reminder concerning the production schedule, listing the various stages of the creative process leading up to the premiere in Châlon-en-Champagne in France in April 2008. This was followed by a review of the technical work schedule for the next few days. The team had just received a sushi conveyor from Switzerland, an item that will be explored during the course of the week, but some parts were missing. If all goes well, it should be operational by Wednesday.

Robert Lepage then described the artistic project: *The Blue Dragon* was born of the desire to return to an exploration of the universe of *The Dragons' Trilogy*. At that time in the mid-1980s (as indicated in the prologue to *The Dragons' Trilogy*), none of the creative team had ever been to China.

In 2002 when the decision was made to remount *The Dragons' Trilogy*, the context had changed. Ex Machina had presented a number of performances in Asia, especially Hong Kong. That led to a new perception of Asia, one that Lepage now wished to incorporate into the play.

An initial work session took place in January 2007 when Robert Lepage travelled to Shanghai with Marie Michaud for a direct experience of the city. Shortly after their return, a small team began to explore the impressions and ideas stimulated by the trip to Asia.

Lepage wants to retain the character of Pierre Lamontagne from *The Dragons' Trilogy*. Now living in Shanghai, he is fifty years of age and owns an art gallery in Mogashan, a neighbourhood that is a hub of contemporary art in China. Lamontagne's main interest is works by young Chinese artists. The second character is a Canadian named Claire who is in China on a business trip. For the moment, it seems that she is also motivated by the desire to adopt a Chinese baby.

During this second phase of the work, the team hopes to rummage through the universe of Hergé's comic book *The Blue Lotus*. For many in the creative team, their first contact with China was reading the adventures of Tintin in childhood (the comic strip panel format may very well influence the set design). They also want to study the Chinese art market (particularly a flourishing industry in producing knockoffs of Old Masters) and the world of tattooing. Several items will be used in these explorations, such as the sushi conveyor, stationary bicycles, videos and music. In the room are a number of props and costumes that will be used in improvisations.

The Four Dragons

For *The Dragons' Trilogy* and *The Blue Dragon*, Ex Machina opted for an interpretation of Chinese mythology whereby the four dragons symbolize the cycle of the seasons. *The Dragons' Trilogy* consisted of three parts: the green dragon, the red dragon and the white dragon. *The Blue Dragon* now completes the cycle.

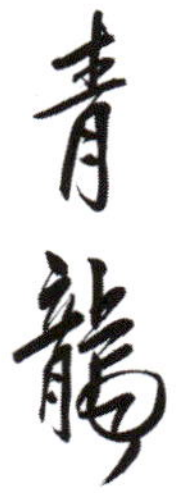

The Green Dragon
The green dragon brings life, lives in water and is associated with the spring. He represents youth.

The Red Dragon
The symbol of war and combat, the red dragon lives on land and is associated with the summer. He represents adulthood.

The White Dragon
This is the flying dragon, associated with the autumn. He represents the wisdom of the twilight years.

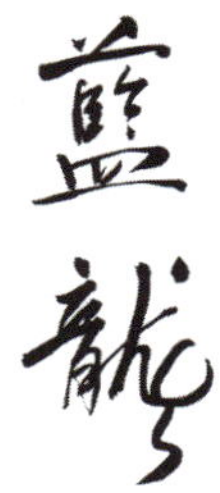

The Blue Dragon
This dragon lives under the snow and is associated with winter. He represents death and rebirth. An invisible creature, he is generally represented as a blue flame and appears in the form of lightning.

Calligraphy: Truong Chanh Trung

MONDAY, JUNE 18

Evening Work Session

Good news! The missing parts of the sushi conveyor arrived sooner than expected, and the technical team was able to assemble the device this afternoon. Of a relatively simple mechanical design, the system suggests a number of interesting possibilities. For the moment, it resembles a stainless steel counter eight metres long and not quite one metre wide. Underneath the counter, a motor drives a series of magnets. Powered by magnetic force, metallic objects slide along the surface of the conveyor. The evening began with initial experiments with the conveyor.

After amusing themselves testing the possibilities of the conveyor by tossing every metal object on hand onto the device, Robert Lepage and Marie Michaud felt it was time to use the machine in an improvisation. Dishes, glasses, chopsticks – after a few minutes, the stage has been turned into a sushi restaurant.

Lepage and Michaud are not yet certain about the relationship between Pierre and Claire. How long have they known each other? Are they friends? Have they ever been lovers? Does their emotional bond prevent Claire from adopting a child? On the other hand, what if the two protagonists have never met? For the first improvisation, the actors start with the idea that this is the first time they have ever met. Bit by bit, out of the improvised scene a past emerges, as well as the ambitions of each character.

A miniature camera was placed on the sushi conveyor, and video was gradually integrated into the following explorations. While the exact content of the play remains unknown, it is quite apparent that at least one scene will take place in a sushi restaurant.

Preparing the sushi conveyor.
Photo: David Leclerc

Each experiment is meticulously described on paper, and filmed by assistant director Félix Dagenais.
Photo: David Leclerc

Studies for a video self-portrait of Marie Michaud.
Photo: David Leclerc

Robert Lepage and Marie Michaud prepare the ground for an improvisation.
Photo: David Leclerc

Marie Michaud and Robert Lepage each improvise the character of Sue Ming. Here Robert Lepage plays the young Chinese artist in the vernissage scene.
Photo: David Leclerc

TUESDAY, JUNE 19

Morning Work Session

The morning was spent defining the motivations and ambitions of the characters. Since the January work session, Marie Michaud has been conducting research on China and the issue of international adoption. The new criteria established by the Chinese government are much stricter than before. The adoptive parents' living conditions, health and social status are now examined in great detail. One imagines that Claire's desire to adopt a Chinese baby is now impossible under the new regulations.

TUESDAY, JUNE 19

Evening Work Session

Marie Michaud presented a chart outlining all the diverse relationships possible between the characters. Each avenue explored tells a different story. In discussing the matter, Lepage and Michaud realized that the situation calls for a third character for the story to evolve, and they began to wonder what sort of person that would be. Initial feelers seem to indicate a young Chinese artist, who is temporarily named Sue Ming. The story soon takes on new life. She and Pierre were once lovers. Maybe she is pregnant and wants to be rid of the baby. Claire, of course, is interested in having the child. The new triangle generates new dramatic conflicts.

WEDNESDAY, JUNE 20

The previous day was spent discussing, comparing ideas and trying to define the issues. It has left in its wake an irrepressible desire for further exploration. Luckily enough, without prior consultation everyone has shown up with objects likely to produce an interesting effect on the sushi conveyor. The morning was spent playing with model trains, Chinese junks, Tintin figurines, etc.

Back in the room that evening, Michel Gauthier presented a scale model he built of the Transrapid in Shanghai, a high speed magnetic levitation train. It suits the conveyor perfectly. Lepage immediately wanted to test the possibilities of this new toy. Using video, a few tricks of perspective and the Transrapid scale model, he was able to create the illusion of a full-size train entering the station while Claire waits on the platform. After playing with this new discovery for a few minutes he said, "Very nice, but now let's see what sort of perversions this can lead to!" With a few deft manipulations, he changed the perspective and created the illusion on the screen that Claire was seated in the model train. By means of small objects, illusions of perspective, video, comic strips, movement and character, the vocabulary of the piece gradually takes shape.

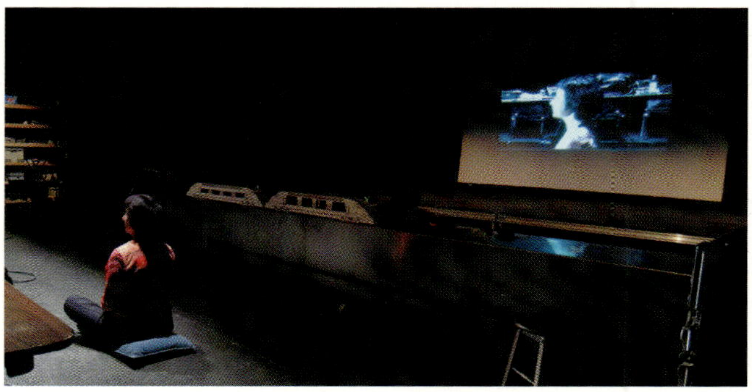

Integrating the various component elements of the play. The model train on the sushi conveyor enters the station, while the video creates the illusion that Claire is on board. (Marie Michaud)
Photo: David Leclerc

(Left: Marie Michaud. Centre: Michel Gauthier and Patrick Caux.
Right: Robert Lepage and Michel Gauthier)
Photo: David Leclerc

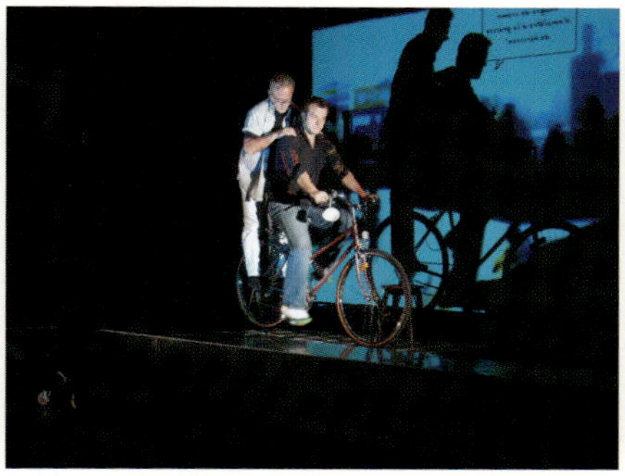

THURSDAY, JUNE 21

The team explored various ways of recreating a bicycle ride along the streets of Shanghai, as though Pierre and Claire were visiting the city. There is also the possibility of Pierre and Sue Ming enjoying a romantic ride together. These scenes evoke the codes of the comic book, as the direction the bicycle is heading suggests time travel. When the bicycle faces stage left, the audience follows the evolving story. When it faces stage right, it is as though we are travelling back in time. This thus offers the possibility of exploring memories, dreams and symbols.

FRIDAY, JUNE 22

Among the ideas conjured up during the week, an especially interesting one is the fact that China is a past master in the art of imitation and replication. Watching documentaries and news reports on Chinese commercial practice indicates that the notion of intellectual property is often unknown and/or ignored in Chinese industry. The team has identified an entire neighbourhood, Dafen, where hundreds of copyists reproduce the works of the great masters.

Throughout the week, the idea of situating the action of *The Blue Dragon* in two different time periods was explored. The first part of the story would take place the year before the 2008 Olympic Games in Beijing, with the second half taking place in the year following the sports event. During a second trip to China, Claire is searching for Sue Ming, who now lives in Dafen. She has abandoned original art work and now earns her living making copies of paintings.

Dafen – A Silent Scene

This scene was mounted in a few minutes. Robert Lepage promptly announced it to be complete as is, and it will most likely be integrated in full into the performance.

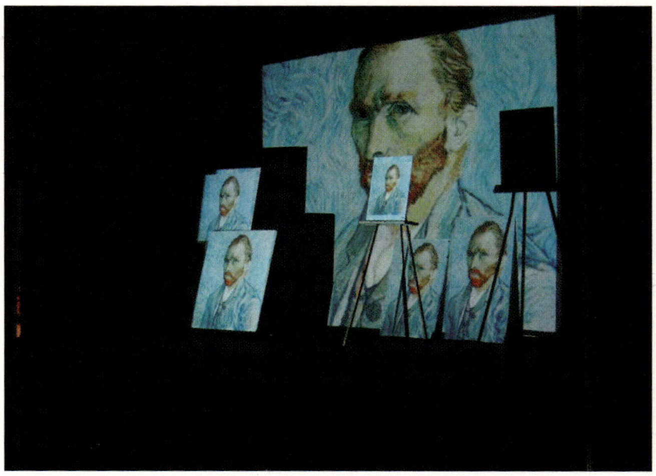

Video solution to illustrate the work of the copyists in Dafen. The blank canvas gradually fills with multiple copies of Van Gogh's self-portrait.
Photo: David Leclerc

SATURDAY, JUNE 23

The June work session ended with a synthesis. Elements have fallen into place but many unknown factors remain. Ground must be prepared, situations clarified. Based on the scenes developed during the week, Lepage is ready to present an initial version of the story. The next work session is scheduled for October at the Caserne.

Order of Scenes
(after two weeks of work)

1 - **(Opening credits) Pierre gets a tattoo.**
2 - **(Prologue) Child of the world –** Claire's application for adoption denied.
3 - **Airport** – Claire arrives in Shanghai. She has lost her suitcase.
4 - **Pierre's home** – Combination workshop and apartment.
5 - **Taxi** – Pierre and Sue Ming listen to a soap opera on the radio.
6 - **Boutique** – Claire shops for clothes. She is fascinated by tiny Chinese dolls.
7 - **Paintings** – Pierre and Sue Ming hang paintings for an exhibit.
8 - **Sushi Train** – Ideological conflict between Pierre and Claire.
9 - **Sales Pitch** – Claire presents a marketing strategy for a new line of sportswear. At an art fair in Beijing, Pierre presents the work of his artists.
10 - **Vernissage** – Claire and Sue Ming meet for the first time.
11 - **Bicycles** – Claire and Sue Ming go for a bicycle ride in Shanghai (no dialogue).
12 - **Zoo** – Claire and Sue Ming view the pandas. Claire learns that Sue Ming is pregnant.
13 - **Pregnancy test –** Claire and Sue Ming.
14 - **Bicycle** – Pierre is on a solo bicycle ride. Images evoked: the love affair between Pierre and Sue Ming, Shanghai as seen by Pierre (i.e. à la *Blue Lotus*).

Olympics

15 - **Hong Kong** – Claire returns to China.
16 - **Dafen** – Claire finds Sue Ming in her copyist's workshop. Claire discovers the baby.
17 - **Train** – Claire goes to meet Pierre in Shanghai to tell him that he is a father.
18 - **A Park in Shanghai** – Pierre practises tai chi.

Sketch by set designer Michel Gauthier.

Part 2 / Opera – The Voice of Hypertheatre

BY BERNARD GILBERT

THE COMING TOGETHER OF EX MACHINA AND THE WORLD OF OPERA OCCURRED GRADUALLY, MUCH LIKE TWO INDIVIDUALS WHO FIRST NOTICE ONE ANOTHER AND THEN HOVER AROUND EACH OTHER BEFORE DECIDING TO EMBARK ON A RELATIONSHIP. LEPAGE FIRST GOT INVOLVED IN OPERA IN THE 1990s WITH *BLUEBEARD'S CASTLE* AND *ERWARTUNG*. WITH *THE DAMNATION OF FAUST* IN 1999, EX MACHINA PLUNGED INTO ITS FIRST OPERA, AND THE PACE QUICKLY ACCELERATED. ACCORDING TO RICHARD FRÉCHETTE, A LONG-TIME COLLABORATOR, IT WAS INEVITABLE. "ROBERT LEPAGE, EX MACHINA AND OPERA ARE MADE FOR ONE ANOTHER. THE WORLD OF OPERA, THE STAGING POSSIBILITIES… IT WAS ONLY A MATTER OF TIME."

In the opening scene of **1984,** the Royal Opera House soloists and chorus play the members of the party headed by Big Brother (London, 2005).
Photo: Bill Cooper

L' ORFEO
FAVOLA IN MVSICA
DA CLAVDIO MONTEVERDI
RAPPRESENTATA IN MANTOVA
l'Anno 1607. & nouamente data in luce.
AL SERENISSIMO SIGNOR
D. FRANCESCO GONZAGA
Prencipe di Mantoua, & di Monferato, &c.
In Venetia Appresso Ricciardo Amadino.
M D C IX.

Frontispiece of the first edition of *L'Orfeo*, by Claudio Monteverdi, published in 1609. (DR)

Four Centuries in the Blink of an Eye

The birth of opera dates to the early 17th century. The oldest opera in the repertoire, Claudio Monteverdi's *L'Orfeo*, was created in 1607. This art form is the same age as Quebec City.

A marriage of music and theatre, opera incorporates all the performing arts – it is a total or comprehensive art form, as Richard Wagner noted in the 19th century. Performed at court and for the nobility for two centuries, opera eventually became popular in London, where Handel was a star in the early 1700s. Then came Mozart, a monument of the classical period. The 19th century was the golden age of opera, especially in Italy, France and Germany. It made inroads in the Americas late in the century. Over the 175 years from Handel to Puccini, hundreds of works were created and performed on the stages of Europe. The major opera houses are an echo of that era: the Fenice in Venice, La Scala in Milan, the Opéra de Paris, Covent Garden in London, the Vienna Opera, and later, New York City's Metropolitan Opera. Opera became a middle-class fashion in the 20th century but never attracted a mass audience, losing public favour to the musicals of Broadway and London's West End. There has been a perceptible revival of opera since the 1980s, however, with the introduction of elements from the modern theatre, thereby revamping a stultified art form. Ex Machina has been participating in this rejuvenation for the past few years.

Singers are the bedrock of opera, and the best – Callas, Freni, Domingo, Pavarotti and now Netrebko and Villazon – attract adoring fans. Conductors have also become stars, from Toscanini to Karajan and Levine to Barenboim. Renowned Quebec artists include singers Albani, Raoul Jobin, Pierrette Alarie, Léopold Simoneau and Joseph Rouleau, and conductors Wilfred Pelletier and Bernard Labadie.

The Damnation of Faust. Choreographers: Johanne Madore (dance) and Alain Gauthier (acrobatics). Paris, 2001.
Photo: Éric Mahoudeau

"OPERA IS HYPERTHEATRE," OBSERVES ROBERT LEPAGE. "OPERA EXPRESSES THE WIND, THE TIDES, THE COSMOS AND ENERGY ITSELF. IT TAKES US BEYOND SOUND AND LIGHT TOWARDS A DISCOVERY OF THE INVISIBLE DIMENSIONS OF DAILY LIFE. OPERA IS MORE PRONE TO TRAGEDY THAN DRAMA, DELVING INTO ARCHETYPES AND EXCESS. OPERA IS LARGER THAN LIFE."

Nothing More Theatrical than Opera

The human voice is at the heart of the discipline – the singing voice, sonorous and powerful. "Our task is to focus on and highlight the voice," explains Lepage, "to make sure that the set design, the staging and the blocking hinder as little as possible projection of the voice out into the auditorium. We can help, if only by placing the singers downstage and avoiding the use of large fabrics, paintings and curtains, ensuring that they don't sing to the stage or the wings. We don't always succeed, but we must aim for that ideal situation."

Opera demands oversized voices, an exalted style that runs counter to truth. The voice is the central point from which an entire world of emotion radiates. Opera is the realm of archetypes, a place where gods, demigods and other heroes live out their lives.

Der Ring des Nibelungen, the Wagner Ring cycle that Ex Machina will be producing at the Metropolitan Opera in New York from 2010 to 2012, is at the heart of this dynamic. The *Ring* is to opera what The Great Work is to alchemy. Love, emotion, ambition and power are incarnated by the music and the characters in a drama that borrows from Greek tragedy and the founding myths of the Germanic peoples. It is a story based on the interaction of the natural elements, especially water and fire. It is a tale of gods claiming the power to dominate the earth, an ultimately impossible quest.

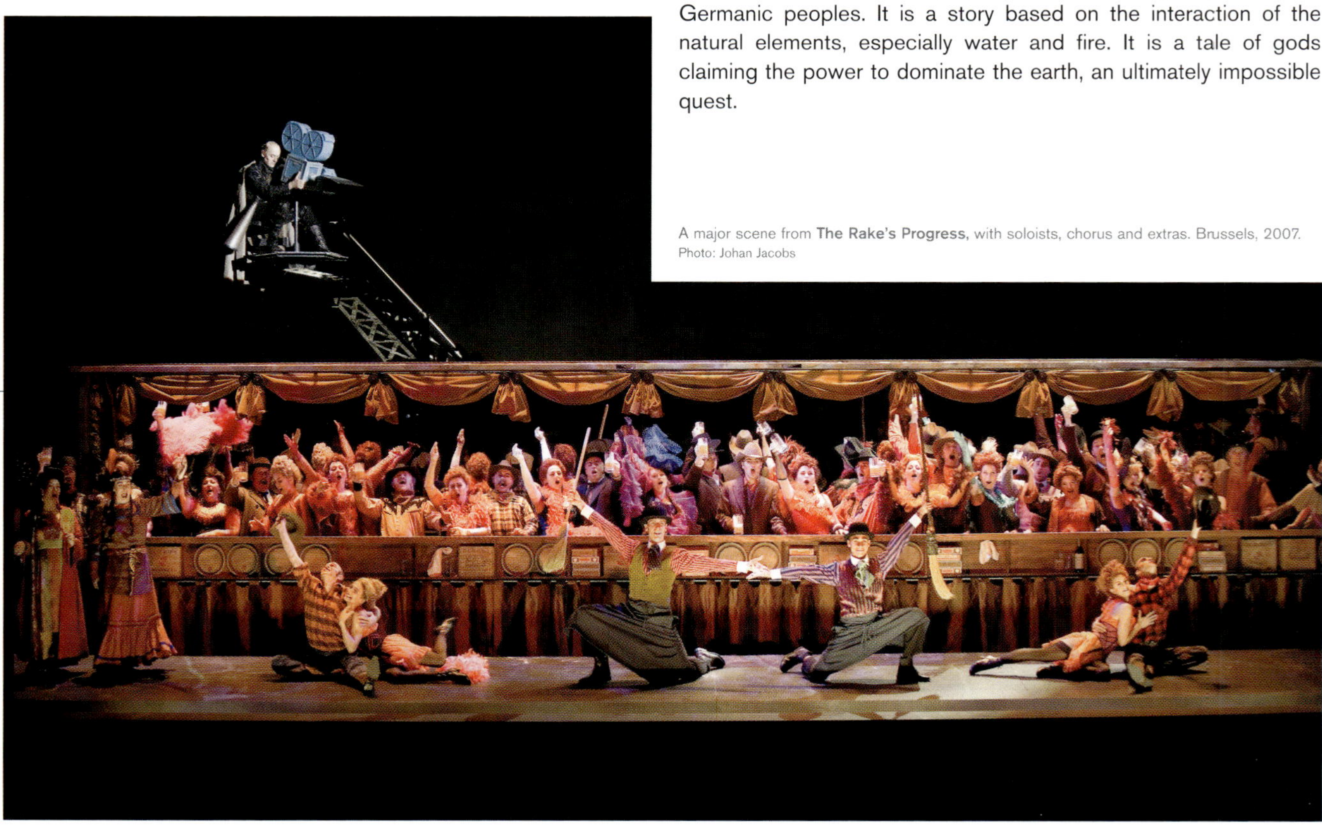

A major scene from **The Rake's Progress**, with soloists, chorus and extras. Brussels, 2007.
Photo: Johan Jacobs

Cio Cio San, the heroine of Puccini's *Madama Butterfly*, is 15 years old. The musical score calls for a mature soprano with extensive opera experience, much like the great 20th century Spanish opera singer Victoria de Los Angeles. Verisimilitude is of secondary importance. (DR)

The Supernatural Voice

In opera, voice classification ranges from the high-pitched to the low-pitched. The four registers for the female voice are soprano, mezzo soprano, alto and contralto. There are five registers for male voices: counter tenor, tenor, baritone, bass baritone and bass.
Each register is rated according to tessitura or range, agility, timbre or tone and projection, the parameters that determine the repertoire. There are thus coloratura or dramatic sopranos, buffo or heroic tenors (heldentenors), the high or lyric baritone, etc. Each era has its own conventions, assigning registers to different character types. The main love interests will be a soprano and a tenor, the father figure will be a bass, and the heroine's servant a mezzo soprano. The principal criterion in choosing a performer is his or her vocal register, followed by a physical resemblance to the character or acting talent.

Rebecca Blankenship (left) sang the role of the troubled heroine of **Erwartung** for the Canadian Opera Company in Toronto. She also performed in **The Seven Streams of the River Ota,** and in the collective theatre piece **Lipsynch.**
Photo: Michael Cooper

First Forays into Opera

The first steps taken by Robert Lepage into the world of opera occurred in Toronto in 1993. While Ex Machina was not involved, the double bill of *Bluebeard's Castle* (Béla Bartók) and *Erwartung* (Arnold Schoenberg) presented by the Canadian Opera Company was impressive. It has since been performed in Asia, Europe and North America, including the Opéra de Montréal (2004) and the Opéra de Québec (2008).
Consisting of two short works requiring only three soloists and a group of acrobats/dancers (these pieces do not have a chorus), it was an ideal project for an initial adventure. Lepage had a few doubts as to how to approach the world of opera. Were all the singers divas? Would they be able to act, and be open to direction? Is the conductor's interest limited to the music? These fears were laid to rest after this first experience.
In conjunction with set designer Michael Levine, Robert Lepage created two very singular worlds – that of the mystery surrounding the disappearance of Bluebeard's wives, and the dismantling of reality that Schoenberg exploited in *Erwartung*, a piece about madness. These two post-romantic, expressionistic works were composed in 1918 and 1909. Rife with images of figures suddenly emerging from the walls or from the back of the stage as though weightless, and images projected simultaneously from different points of view, they are typical of Lepage's stage language.
Opera first made an appearance in an Ex Machina work in *The Seven Streams of the River Ota* (1994). A German opera singer character, played by mezzo soprano Rebecca Blankenship, sings a Puccini aria and a few songs by Francis Poulenc, a 20th century French composer.

Muybridge's famous photo montage used in the procession scene. Paris, 2001.
Photo: Opéra national de Paris

The Damnation of Faust – *A Long-term Project*

Created in 1999 at the Saito Kinen festival in Matsumoto, Japan and remounted at the Opéra de Paris Bastille in 2001, 2004 and 2006, *The Damnation of Faust* by the French composer Hector Berlioz was the company's first opera. The piece is not an opera *per se*, but rather a concert stage piece. Termed a "dramatic legend" by Berlioz, it was first presented as a concert version in Paris in 1846. It has since been presented as both a concert version and as a full stage production. The prestigious Catalan company La Fura del Baus presented its own version of *The Damnation* at the Salzburg Festival one month before the premiere in Matsumoto, an indication of the timeless qualities of the piece. Thus two avant-garde theatre companies simultaneously tackled the opera version of a legend that dates from the Middle Ages.

The Ex Machina version of *The Damnation of Faust* was inspired by imagery from the 19th century, the composer's own era. In the prologue, Faust, fascinated by science, takes a book from his library. The staging, which lures the audience into the book, is based on a fully vertical set design with a scaffold divided into 24 panels (evoking 24 frames per second) rising four levels high. In the late 19th century, thanks in part to the advent of photography, people like Eadweard Muybridge used photos in their scientific research, thereby laying the groundwork for cinema. An elliptic tale written at a time when the laws governing the kinetics of moving pictures were being discovered, *The Damnation* called for cinematic language. Using a system of mobile screens and mirror cubes, the set became a screen of dreams for images projected onto both front and rear surfaces.

With *The Damnation*, Ex Machina aimed to push the limits of existing technology, and with each new remount, it was possible to pursue more such research. The transition from Matsumoto to Paris allowed for the use of high-definition imagery. For presentations at the Metropolitan Opera of New York in 2008 and 2009, the company used interactive video, working with the German designer Holger Förterer.

As Robert Lepage notes, interactive video offers an extension of living art. "In *The Damnation* and even more in Wagner's *Ring of the Nibelungen*, the visual effects will be triggered by diverse parameters, including the actors' voices. These effects can be provoked by the texture, register or timbre of the voice, or by certain chords or melodic progressions, and perhaps by the instruments in the orchestra. In opera, that is the best way to integrate the visual approach – let the voice and the music decide. The voice is at the heart of the piece." Interactions between performers and projected imagery will also be generated by onstage movements captured by infrared or by laser light.

Soprano Susan Graham and tenor Giuseppe Sabbatini rehearse **The Damnation of Faust** with Robert Lepage. Matsumoto, 1999.
Photo: Grand Stage Matsumoto 1999 Report

From Idea to Performance

The development of opera projects at Ex Machina follows a logic similar to that pursued in the company's theatre pieces. The main difference is the time available – contracts for opera singers are sometimes signed five years before the premiere – and the fact that the musical score already exists and need not be composed. The former Dalhousie fire station is once again headquarters for research and development.

The approach to each opera is fleshed out during an initial series of meetings attended by at least the director and the set designer. They discuss the general staging concept, the main lines and arcs of the set and the era in which the story will take place. The process is nourished by diverse sources of inspiration: the music and theme of the opera, books about the composer and the era he lived in, photos, documents, films and specific objects.

The conceptual elements behind the Ex Machina opera projects are often derived from research on the physical organization of the stage space. (Mention was made earlier of the vertical set of 24 boxes employed in *The Damnation of Faust*.) For *1984*, the spatial concept consisted of three triangles forming a square, all of it included in two quarter-circles pivoting on a 360° rail. Various arrangements of these items allowed for the creation of the different locations where the story takes place. For *The Rake's Progress*, establishing a dynamic relationship between the raked stage and a huge panoramic screen required extensive work sessions. For the double program of *The Nightingale / Reynard the Fox*, Asian water puppets act as a foil to African-inspired shadow theatre.

Once the concept becomes clear, the design team expands. In order to pursue development and to validate ideas, workshops with prototypes are organized at the Caserne: sections of the set, the main props, research on projection and lighting, costume fittings, etc. The main outline of the staging is determined at this point, and working with these prototypes is a form of raw, direct playwriting. For *The Nightingale / Reynard the Fox* project three workshops were held over an eight-month period, whereas for the Wagner Ring cycle, the sessions took place over an almost three-year period.

Anne driving her vehicle. The role was performed in Quebec City by the dancer Rosalie Trudel and in Brussels by the soprano Laura Claycomb. Background images by Boris Firquet. Two different images of the vehicle as it appeared in **The Rake's Progress.**
Photos: David-Alexandre Chabot and Johan Jacobs

After these workshops comes a six- to eight-month construction period, which involves many suppliers and specialized workers. Building the sets requires substantial means. The floor structure, beams, girders and walls are built using leading-edge industrial techniques, and the floor coverings and wall finishes are often products originally developed for professional sports. A number of manufacturing and assembly techniques – industrial handicraft, as it were – are used in building a unique stage setting.
The team verifies movements or tests configurations at various key stages of development. The patina and the props are added in the final phase, making the set design come alive, and the costumes and the video imagery are also crafted at this point. The team then leaves Quebec City to present the premiere of the play in the designated locale. Transporting the set for *1984* required four shipping containers.
After the set-up, it's time for rehearsals – where the singers, actors-dancers-acrobats and members of the chorus find themselves on stage at last. During a previous two- to three-week period, the director, his assistant and several designers have already staged the presentation in the rehearsal hall. Final touches are now made to the sets, the video, the wigs and makeup, and the props. The cast is usually onstage two weeks before the premiere. Everything is finally assembled – the cast, the set, the orchestra, the lighting and special effects – for a complete spectacle.
For Ex Machina opening night marks the end of a theatrical adventure, and most of the collaborators involved in creating the piece return home the next day. After a few years of work, from initial idea to pre-production to polished performance, the task has been accomplished. Then again, not quite.
"Given the vagaries and mishaps inherent in the presentation, every night at the opera is unique," says Robert Lepage: soloists can fall ill, which is why many opera houses hire understudies who can replace them at a moment's notice; a member of the chorus, an acrobat or a dancer might be sick or injured. These unforeseen factors can affect both the staging and the performance.
Ex Machina considers it essential to monitor how a performance evolves: the lighting and costume designers often help in that regard and, if his schedule allows, Robert Lepage will attend performances to hone and polish the piece, to push it a bit further. While the strictures of the operatic form are greater than in theatre, repeat performances allow for additional creative experimentation.

The Damnation of Faust a few days before the premiere. Matsumoto, 1999.
Photos: Grand Stage Matsumoto 1999 Report

Set Construction

The development and exploration work carried out at the Caserne is essential to the process of staging the opera. In the first image of *1984* below, the team projects (on cylindrical walls mounted on a rail) video images of Jacques Collin and Lionel Arnould while a dancer plays the role of Winston. In the second photo Robert Lepage and set designer Carl Fillion discuss the use of a large apron designed to cover the rear of the set. In order to get a better view, they are standing in the street behind the main studio.

Supervised by technical director Michel Gosselin, the set construction firm Scène Éthique (clients include Céline Dion and the Cirque du Soleil) assemble set pieces. The company built the sets for *The Damnation of Faust* and *The Rake's Progress*.

Photos: Jacques Collin

Sketches by François Barbeau of the libertine Tom Rakewell.

Sources of Inspiration for The Rake's Progress

In June 2005, Robert Lepage showed up at the first work session with a book about Las Vegas. Attending the meeting were set designer Carl Fillion, lighting designer Etienne Boucher, technical director Michel Gosselin and production manager Bernard Gilbert. Using the book as a starting point, the team began establishing links between 18th-century London as portrayed in William Hogarth's eight paintings (the direct source of inspiration for the composer and his librettists) and the period when the opera was written (1951). Stravinsky was living in Hollywood at the time, hoping to write for film or television. The themes of the opera are prostitution, gambling and moral downfall, which led to the decision that Ex Machina's version of *The Rake's Progress* should take place in the era in which it was written. Costume designer François Barbeau suggested several films from the 1950s and 1960s for the team to view, which became another source of inspiration.

The Ex Machina version of *The Rake's Progress* shifted considerably from the original libretto, which was true to Hogarth's London. Inspired by post-war American cinema, the set design included a large panoramic screen upstage. The main element of the set is a huge raked floor from which emerge most of the story elements: Nick Shadow, a film studio, a star's trailer, Anne Trulove's family home, her car, Leicester Square in London, a swimming pool, a cemetery and an asylum.

The storyboards prepared by assistant director Neilson Vignola are incredibly specific, as indicated by the notes for this scene in the first act of **The Rake's Progress,** with all the component elements on the same page.

ACTE: 1	Scène: 2- Bordel chez Mother Goose (Studio de cinéma des années 50 aux USA)	Durée: 12:45 (Intro : 01:00 / Finale: 00 :25)	QUAND: 19:30 à 32:15

DÉCORS:
- Studio de cinéma : Décor western — Cyclo — 1 Grue de cinéma — 4 Pantographes
- 1 Bar — 1 Mur de miroirs — 1 Podium 3 marches au lointain (apparition du Chœur)

QUI: (Costumes) (49 Artistes sur scène + 1 Technicien)
- Tom — Shadow — Mother Goose — 4 membres de l'équipe de tournage (Figurants/es)
- 2 Entraîneuses bagarreuses (Figurantes) — 2 Clients bagarreurs (Figurants) — 18 F Entraîneuses/Clientes du Saloon (Choristes)
- 18 H Clients du Saloon (Choristes) — 2 Barman (Figurants) — 1 Grutier **(Technicien)**

MOUVEMENTS SUR SCÈNE:
- **TRANSITION:** **Ouverture** du plancher qui devient un mur de miroirs **& Apparition** d'un Bar du plancher ouvert
- **Sortie** du Derrick vers Cour **& Entrée** de la Grue de cinéma de Jardin
- **Descente** des Équipements d'éclairage cinéma sur 3 pantographes des cintres à la Face
- **PENDANT LA SCÈNE:** **Apparition** de Tom, assis sur la grue, au dessus du mur miroir
- **Pivotements** fréquents de la grue de cinéma, avec Shadow assis dessus, tout au long de la scène
- **Installation** du lit, drap et coussins sur scène, caché derrière le mur de miroirs
- **Disparition** aux cintres des 3 Pantographes de la face **& Apparition** de 1 du lointain
- **Disparition** du bar dans le plancher **& Fermeture** du plancher mur de miroirs
- **Disparition** de Mother Goose et de Tom, avec le drap et coussins, par le centre du Matelas en Coeur

ACCESSOIRES:
- 1 Bouteille d'alcool à casser — 1 Grue de cinéma — 1 Caméra de cinéma — 4 Pantographes
- 6 Projecteurs de cinéma (dont 1x5K) — ? Bouteilles pour servir (Barman) — 20 bocks à bière — 2 Chiffons (Barman)
- Étuis à revolvers & Revolvers (Ch.+Fig.) — ? Montres de poche (Choristes) — ? Sacoches (Choristes) — 1 Paire de lunette (Shadow)
- 1 Matelas trafiqué en forme de cœur — 1 Drap (en satin) pour le matelas — 5 Coussins — 1 Gaffe d'électricien
- Divers Équipements de cinéma : Trousse maquillage + 1 clap de cinéma + 1 chrono + 1 Calepin de note

ÉCLAIRAGE:
- Éclairage de plateau de cinéma sur Pantographes — Éclairage venant du plancher derrière le comptoir du bar
- Feux de la rampe encastrée sur le devant du plateau — Éclairage des pantographes pour la zone du Lit et du Bar
- Rampe de lumières sur les torses du Chœur au lointain

PROJECTIONS: Quoi — Où
-

EFFETS SPÉCIAUX:
- Tom se fait soulever par l'ouverture du plancher — Bouteille cassée sur la tête d'un figurant
- Disparition de Mother Goose et de Tom par le matelas au centre-cour du plateau avec coussins, drap et chapeau

MUSIQUE / EFFETS SONORES:
- 12 coups de l'horloge (fait par l'orchestre)

Titre: Act 1, Scene 2	Sujet: Storyboard Technique	Last date modified : 05-12-06 21:10
Auteur: Neilson Vignola	The Rake's Progress	Page 1 of 1
Macintosh HD:Users:BERT:Bert 21022007:EM livre 2007:Choix 23022007:RakeTSB_Act1Sc2.doc		

Nancy Gustafson as Julia and Simon Keenlyside as Winston in **1984.** London, 2005.
Photo: Bill Cooper

The Ex Machina Operas

Ex Machina does not necessarily intend to tackle canons of the opera repertoire such as *La Traviata* or *Carmen*. The company began its work in the genre with little known works (*Bluebeard's Castle / Erwartung*) or pieces that are not technically operas (*The Damnation of Faust*). It then received commissions for specific works such as *1984*, by the composer and conductor Lorin Maazel. The fact that this piece could be created from the ground up was a decisive factor in its selection. The Théâtre Royal de la Monnaie in Brussels later offered Robert Lepage the chance to select an opera from a choice of four lesser known works, which included *The Rake's Progress* by Stravinsky. Given its growing success in the field, the company is increasingly able to choose the operas it wishes to mount.

The project to produce a double bill of *The Nightingale* and *Reynard the Fox*, two short operas also composed by Stravinsky, was the result of an expression of interest by Robert Lepage: *The Nightingale* is an adaptation of an Andersen tale he knew well; *Reynard* is a burlesque meant to be sung and acted. In this production Ex Machina wanted to explore the world of marionettes and American designer Michael Curry and Quebec designer Martin Genest combined their efforts on these projects, taking their inspiration from Vietnamese water puppets for the Andersen tale, and shadow theatre for *Reynard*.

A major project for 2010-2012, a new production at the Metropolitan Opera in New York of Richard Wagner's *Der Ring des Nibelungen* marks a return to commissioned work. Producing this classic in such a renowned opera house is a sign that Ex Machina is held in high regard indeed. The *Ring* project will take place over a five-year period.

These works (all written after 1850) incorporate ideas that correspond perfectly to the theatre repertoire of Ex Machina. A popular device in theatre, the idea of the double resurfaces – the devil appearing twice, two double programs, two Stravinsky projects. The very cinematic idea of movement with multiple points of view is present in both opera and theatre. There is a reference in *The Nightingale* to the Danish writer Andersen, the subject of *The Andersen Project*. With the *Ring*, there is once again the attraction of lengthy epics. The theatre and opera projects of Ex Machina are mutually enriching, if only in terms of the expertise acquired, which advances from one production to the next.

Walhalla, residence of the gods, as portrayed in the production presented at the Metropolitan Opera since the late 1980s. The performances of the **Ring** as directed by Otto Schenk concluded in spring 2009, giving way to the Ex Machina version.
Photo: Ken Howard

Opera Houses

The relationship that Ex Machina maintains with opera houses is worthy of note, given that their respective working methods are at opposite extremes. The Ex Machina style, with its workshops and the dynamic collaborative energy of its studio, provides a bracing jolt for opera houses, whose expertise is based on centuries-old traditions. As Bernard Poccroulle noted when he was director of the Théâtre Royal de la Monnaie in Brussels, "It is important to cultivate opportunities to create synergies between opera houses, whose production methods are particular and sometimes unwieldy, and creative companies like Ex Machina. Projects like these are very good for opera. I must say that in that regard, our collaboration with Ex Machina was exemplary."[11] With opera houses, the company has access to extraordinary expertise in a variety of trades, as the houses are often equipped with reputable workshops for building sets, props, costumes and wigs. Conversely, the Ex Machina creative process and the extensive workshops at the Caserne exceed the showcase development capacity of opera houses. Another aspect of note is that video is an essential element in the company's opera productions, an art form that is rarely put to use in opera. Ex Machina thus obliges opera houses to develop expertise in new technologies. The coming together of these two worlds leads to innovative and exciting results.

Further exploring these seemingly opposed worlds, the Opéra de Québec and Ex Machina now often collaborate on several different levels. Through this creative exchange, the opera company calls many conventions into question, renews its approach and enriches the art form. For Ex Machina, the relationship provides an opportunity to present new possibilities for productions in Quebec City in the future.

In the last scene of **The Rake's Progress,** Tom Rakewell, performed by Andrew Kennedy, believes he is Adonis. Behind him are his fellow patients at the psychiatric hospital. Brussels, 2007.
Photo: Johan Jacobs

11. Public commentary on *The Rake's Progress*, Brussels, April 2007.

A Rarefied Art Form

A few years ago, Robert Lepage decided to mount fewer pieces from the classical repertoire in order to focus more on creating new works. Opera, however, is an exception to that rule. "Opera entails fewer constraints in terms of subtext and the writer's intentions, for in opera the intentions are apparent in the music. And because the text is sung, it establishes a necessary distance. In fact, realism in opera is, to all intents and purposes, impossible. Whether one looks at Brecht, Mnouchkine or others, the quality of their work relies in part on the fact that they modify the voice. In what I consider to be the most successful theatre plays, not one phrase is pronounced by an ordinary, realistic or normal voice. Considerable research and exploration have been carried out as regards pronunciation, timbre and register. With the singing voice, that heightened state is present at the outset. I find that very interesting."

Another aspect of opera that interests Ex Machina is that it brings together on stage all the artistic disciplines: song and music, dramaturgy, theatre, dance and acrobatics, architecture and the visual arts, video and cinema. It embraces an incredible variety of artists, performers and artisans. This confluence is very much in line with company's philosophy.

For Robert Lepage, "Opera and the cinema are poles apart. Film evokes the world of industry and commerce and is addressed to the masses. In opera, performances are rare and are presented in specialized theatres, attracting far fewer people than movies. Opera is only possible in a sort of box where the relationship between the scene on stage and the audience touches on an essential truth."

The last scene of **The Damnation of Faust.** Marguerite ascends into heaven. Paris, 2001.
Photo: Éric Mahoudeau

The hero of **1984,** Winston Smith (played by baritone Simon Keenlyside), is tortured in Room 101. London, 2005.
Photo: Bill Cooper

THE EX MACHINA TEAM

Robert Lepage
President
Artistic Director
Director

Michel Bernatchez
Producer

Lynda Beaulieu
Agent & Assistant to the President

Jean-Pierre Vézina
Vice-President, Finance

- **Valérie Lambert** — Assistant Producer
- **Louise Roussel** — Production Manager; Tour Manager – Theatre
  - **Marie-Pierre Gagné** — Production Assistant
  - **Paul Bourque** — Production & Technical Assistant
  - **Félix Dagenais** — Assistant Director
  - **Tobie Horswill** — Technical Designer, R&D
  - **Marc-Antoine Fleury** — Network Administrator
- **Bernard Gilbert** — Production Manager – Opera
  - **Vivianne Paradis** — Assistant – Opera
  - **Johanne Tremblay** — Assistant Manager
  - **Catherine Guay** — Project Manager – Opera; Assistant, R&D
- **Martine Rochon** — Communications & Public Relations Director; Production Manager – Publishing
  - **Ève-Alexandra Saint-Laurent** — Project Manager – Publishing
  - **Francis Beaulieu** — Assistant to Artistic Director
- **Francine Poitras** — Assistant to Vice-President, Finance
- **Patrick Durnin** — Technical Director
  - **Micheline Beaulieu** — Archives Manager
  - **Joëlle Cloutier** — Archivist
  - **Sophie Martin** — Rentals Coordinator
  - **Daniel Bernatchez** — Building Maintenance
- **Guy Lanteigne** — Administration & Human Resources
  - **Sylvie Racine** — Administrative Assistant
  - **Francine Dupuis** — Travel Agent & Receptionist
  - **Virginie Leclerc** — Administrative Clerk

BANU, Georges. "L'acteur qui ne revient pas. Journées de théâtre au Japon." Paris: Folio essays, 1993.

BRECHT, Bertolt. *Journals: 1934-1955*. New York: Routledge, 1993.

BRECHT, Bertolt. *Petit organon pour le théâtre*. Paris: L'Arche, 1999.

BROOK, Peter. *L'espace vide. Écrits sur le théâtre*. Paris: Seuil, collection "Point," 1977.

CAMERLAIN, Lorraine (chief editor). *Cahiers de théâtre JEU*, n° 45. Montreal: 1987. Special issue on *La Trilogie des dragons*.

CHAREST, Rémy. *Quelques zones de liberté*. Quebec City: L'instant même and Ex Machina, 1995.

CONNOLLY, L.W., and D.A. HADFIELD. *Canadian Drama and the Critics*. Vancouver: Talonbooks, 1996.

COPEAU, Jacques. "Un essai de rénovation dramatique," in *Registre 1, Appels*. Paris: Gallimard, 1974.

COUTY, Daniel, et al. *Le théâtre*. Paris: Bordas, 1980.

DELGADO, Maria. *In Contact with the Gods*. New York: St. Martin's Press, 1997.

DONOHOE Jr. Joseph, and Jane M. KOUSTAS. *Theater sans frontières: Essays on the Dramatic Universe of Robert Lepage*. East Lansing: Michigan State University Press, 2000.

DUNDJEROVICH, Aleksander. *The Theatricality of Robert Lepage*. Montreal: McGill-Queen's University Press, 2002.

DUNDJEROVICH, Aleksander. *The Cinema of Robert Lepage: The Poetics of Memory*, Director's Cut's series. London: Wallflower Press, 2002.

DUSIGNE, Jean-François. *Le Théâtre du Soleil, des traditions orientales à la modernité occidentale*. Créteil: Centre national de documentation pédagogique, 2003.

FAUCHER, Sophie. *La Casa Azul*. London: Oberon Books Ltd., 2002.

FOUQUET, Ludovic. *Robert Lepage, l'horizon en images*. Quebec City: L'instant même, collection L'instant scène, 2005.

FRICKER, Karen (transcription and comments). *The Seven Streams of the River Ota*. London: Methuen Drama, 1996.

HÉBERT, Chantal, and Irène PERELLI-CONTOS. *La Face cachée du théâtre de l'image*. Quebec City: Presses de l'Université Laval, 2002.

HUXLEY, Michael. *Twentieth Century Performance Reader*. London: Routledge, 2002.

JEAN, Marcel (editor). *Nô*, script of film by Robert Lepage. Quebec City: Les 400 coups, 1998.

JOHNSON, Lise Ann. "Shakespeare's Rapid Eye Movement," in *The Production Notebooks – Theater in Process – Volume II*. New York: Mark Bly, 2001, p. 72-140.

LAVENDER, Andy. *Hamlet in Pieces: Shakespeare Revisited by Robert Brook, Robert Lepage and Robert Wilson*. New York: Continuum Pub Group, 2001.

PIERRON, Agnès. *Dictionnaire de la langue du théâtre*. Paris: Le Robert, 2002.

ROY, Irène. *Le théâtre Repère, du ludique au poétique*. Quebec City: Nuit blanche éditeur, 1994.

SIMON, Sherry. *Le Trafic des langues: traduction et culture dans la littérature québécoise*. Montreal: Boréal, 1994.

STANISLAVSKI, Constantin. N*otes artistiques*. Belfort, Strasbourg, Circé: Théâtre national de Strasbourg, 1997.

TREMBLAY, Michel. Preface to playscript of *La Trilogie des dragons*. Quebec City: Ex Machina and L'instant même, collection L'instant scène, 2005.

WALLACE, Robert. *Producing Marginality*. Saskatoon: Fifth House, 1990.

THEATROGRAPHY (SELECTION)

1979
L'Attaque quotidienne
by Richard Fréchette and Robert Lepage
Théâtre Hummm..., Quebec City

La Ferme des animaux
adaptation of *Animal Farm* by Georges Orwell
Théâtre Hummm..., Quebec City

1980
Saturday Night Taxi
by Richard Fréchette, Francine Lafontaine and Robert Lepage
Théâtre Hummm..., Quebec City

L'École c'est secondaire
by Denis Bernard, Michel Nadeau and Camil Bergeron
Théâtre Repère, Quebec City

1982
À demi-lune
by Johanne Bolduc, Estelle Dutil and Robert Lepage
Théâtre Repère, Quebec City

En attendant
by Richard Fréchette, Jacques Lessard and Robert Lepage
Théâtre Repère, Quebec City

1983
Coriolan et le monstre aux milles têtes
by William Shakespeare
Théâtre Repère, Quebec City

1984
Circulations
by François Beausoleil, Bernard Bonnier, Lise Castonguay and Robert Lepage
Théâtre Repère, Quebec City

1985
La Trilogie des dragons
by Marie Brassard, Jean Casault, Lorraine Côté, Marie Gignac, Robert Lepage and Marie Michaud
Théâtre Repère, Quebec City

À Propos de la demoiselle qui pleurait
by André Jean
Théâtre Repère, Quebec City

Point de fuite
by Robert Lepage
Théâtre Repère, Quebec City

1986
Vinci
by Robert Lepage
Théâtre de Quat'sous, Montreal;
Théâtre Repère, Quebec City

Le Bord extrême
adaptation of *The Seventh Seal* by Ingmar Bergman
Théâtre Repère, Quebec City

1987
Le Polygraphe
by Marie Brassard and Robert Lepage
Théâtre Repère, Quebec City

1988-1991
Les Plaques tectoniques
by Michael Benson, Normand Bissonnette, Céline Bonnier, Boyd Clack, John Cobb, Lorraine Côté, Emma Davie, Richard Fréchette, Sylvie Gagnon, Marie Gignac, Robert Lepage, Michael Levine, François Pick and Jim Twaddale
Théâtre Repère, Quebec City

Le Songe d'une nuit d'été
by William Shakespeare
Théâtre du Nouveau Monde, Montreal

1989
La Vie de Galilée
by Bertolt Brecht
Théâtre du Nouveau Monde, Montreal

Roméo et Juliette
by William Shakespeare
Théâtre Repère, Quebec City;
Night Cap Productions, Saskatoon

1990
La Visite de la vieille dame
by Friedrich Dürrenmatt
Centre National des Arts, Ottawa

1991
Les Aiguilles et l'opium
by Robert Lepage
Les Productions AJP inc.,
Les Productions d'Albert inc.,
Montreal

1992
Le Cycle Shakespeare: Macbeth, Coriolan, La Tempête
by William Shakespeare
(translation and adaptation by Michel Garneau)
Théâtre Repère, Quebec City

A Midsummer's Night Dream
by William Shakespeare
Royal National Theatre, London

1993
National Capitale Nationale
by Jean-Marc Dalpé and Vivian Laxdal
National Arts Centre,
Ottawa

1994
Les Sept Branches de la rivière Ota
by Éric Bernier, Normand Bissonnette, Rebecca Blankenship, Marie Brassard, Anne-Marie Cadieux, Normand Daneau, Richard Fréchette, Marie Gignac, Patrick Goyette, Robert Lepage and Ghislaine Vincent
Ex Machina, Quebec City

1995
Elseneur
based on *Hamlet* by William Shakespeare
Ex Machina, Quebec City

Le Songe d'une nuit d'été
by William Shakespeare
Le Théâtre du Trident, Quebec City

1998
La Géométrie des Miracles
by Tea Alagic, Daniel Bélanger, Jean-François Blanchard, Marie Brassard, Denis Gaudreault, Anthony Howell, Robert Lepage, Kevin McCoy, Thaddeus Phillips, Rodrigue Proteau and Catherine Tardif
Ex Machina, Quebec City

La Tempête
by William Shakespeare
Le Théâtre du Trident, Quebec City

Kindertotenlieder
by Gustav Mahler
Cultural Industry, London

La Celestine
by Fernando de Rojas
Ex Machina, Quebec City;
Kungliga Dramatiska Teatern, Stockholm

1999
Zulu Time
by Jinny Jessica Jacinto, Claire Gignac,
Robert Lepage, Rick Miller, Marco Poulin
and Rodrigue Proteau
Ex Machina, Quebec City

Jean-Sans-Nom
based on the novel by Jules Verne (Adaptation:
Jean Charlebois, music: Robert Charlebois)
Gestion Son Image, Montreal

2000
La Face cachée de la Lune
by Robert Lepage
Ex Machina, Quebec City

2001
La Casa Azul
by Sophie Faucher
Ex Machina, Quebec City

2003
La Trilogie des dragons (nouvelle version)
by Marie Brassard, Jean Casault, Lorraine Côté,
Marie Gignac, Robert Lepage and Marie Michaud
Ex Machina, Quebec City

2004
The Busker's opera
inspired by *The Beggar's Opera* by John Gay
Ex Machina, Quebec City

La Celestina
by Fernando de Rojas
Ex Machina, Quebec City; Ysarca, Spain

2005
Le Projet Andersen
by Robert Lepage
Ex Machina, Quebec City

2007
Lipsynch
by Frédérike Bédard, Carlos Belda,
Rebecca Blankenship, Lise Castonguay, John Cobb,
Nuria Garcia, Marie Gignac, Sarah Kemp,
Robert Lepage, Rick Miller and Hans Piesbergen
Ex Machina, Quebec City

UNDER DEVELOPMENT
Lipsynch
Le Dragon bleu
Eonnagata
Le Moulin à images

OPERAS

1992
Le Château de Barbe-Bleue
opera by Béla Bartók, libretto by Béla Balázs based
on a story by Charles Perrault
Canadian Opera Company, Toronto

Erwartung
opera by Arnold Shœnberg,
libretto by Marie Pappenheim
Canadian Opera Company, Toronto

1999
La Damnation de Faust
by Hector Berlioz, libretto by Hector Berlioz, Almire
Gandonnière and Gérard de Nerval, based on the
poem by Johann Wolfgang von Goethe
Ex Machina, Quebec City;
Festival Saito Kinen, Matsumoto, Japan

2005
1984
by Lorin Maazel, libretto by J. D. McClatchy and
Thomas Meehan, based on the novel by
George Orwell
Ex Machina, Quebec City;
Big Brother Productions, New York

2007
The Rake's Progress
opera in three acts by Igor Stravinsky, libretto by
W.H. Auden and Chester Kallman
Théâtre Royal de la Monnaie, Brussels;
Opéra national de Lyon; San Francisco Opera;
Royal Opera House – Covent Garden, London;
Teatro Real, Madrid

UNDER DEVELOPMENT
Le Rossignol/Renard (1914/1922)
librettos by Igor Stravinsky based on the story by
Hans Christian Andersen and traditional Russian
folk tales

Der Ring des Nibelungen (1876)
theatrical festival in three days, with a Prologue:
Rheingold, *Die Walküre*, *Siegfried*
and *Götterdammerung* by Richard Wagner
Metropolitan Opera, New York

OTHER PROJECTS

1993
Secret World Tour
by Peter Gabriel
Real World Tours, London

2000
Métissages
Musée de la civilisation, Quebec City

2002
Growing Up Tour
by Peter Gabriel
Real World Tours, London

2004
Kà
Cirque du Soleil, Las Vegas

Séoul
Matsumoto
Tsukuba
Tokyo
Nagoya
Kobe
Yamaguchi
Kochi
Taipei
Hong Kong
Singapour
Perth
Adélaïde
Sydney
Wellington